The Light Book

By

Lynn Matheson

The Light Book by Lynn Matheson © 2023

All rights reserved. No part of this book may be used or reproduced in any manner whatsoever, including internet usage, without written permission from Lynn Matheson except in the case of brief quotations embodied in critical articles and reviews.

Independently published in London, England.

Table of Contents

Preface 5

Chapter One: Hypnotherapy 7

Chapter Two: The Womb 25

Chapter Three: Malalia – The First Spirit Guide 31

Chapter Four: Meeting Jesus 81

Chapter Five: Mary Magdalene 93

Chapter Six: The Spirit Council 109

Chapter Seven: Introducing Lucifer 121

Chapter Eight: Life Purpose 139

Chapter Nine: Dealing with Depression and Anxiety ... 149

Chapter Ten: Venus – the Home World 155

Chapter Eleven: The Spirit Council Speaks 159

Chapter Twelve: Reflections 169

Chapter Thirteen: Channelling Malalia 175

Chapter Fourteen: Channelling Jesus 179

Chapter Fifteen: Channelling St Mary 185

Chapter Sixteen: Channelling Lucifer 189

Chapter Seventeen: Channelling the Chinese Sage - Li ... 195

Chapter Eighteen: Channelling African Shaman - Kothiro ... 201

Chapter Nineteen: Channelling Anubis 207

Chapter Twenty: Channelling Kokua 211

Chapter Twenty-one: Meditation for meeting your spirit guides. 217

References 222

Preface

This book grew out of a Life Between Lives Therapy session I had with Scott De Tamble (Lightbetweenlives.com, 2023), a therapist approved by The Michael Newton Institute (Newtoninstitute.org, 2023). The Newton Institute exists to promote the work of Michael Newton, a hypnotherapist who discovered the place between lives where people can visit past lives and meet their soul group and their spirit council. Advice can be given on life's purpose and the meaning of one's existence. Michael Newton has also written books about his work (Newton, 2000, 2002, 2004). My therapy session was a life-changing experience in which I met my spirit guides and my Divine Council. They shared their wisdom with me, and now I want to share it with you.

This book is based on information I was given in my Life Between Lives therapy session and the research I have done later. I have also had channelled sessions with spiritual beings after the session that I have recorded here.

Come back to the light.

CHAPTER ONE:

Hypnotherapy

In 2021 I had a Life Between Lives Therapy session with Scott de *Tamble*. I need to explain what this is. It's a form of hypnotherapy.

I have been interested in hypnotherapy for a long time, and I trained in the therapy myself and practised for years. Let me explain a little about what hypnotherapy is. Hypnotherapy uses hypnosis to change unwanted behaviours. These behaviours could be bad habits, depression, anxiety, phobias, smoking, or eating too much. Hypnosis has been practised in one form or another for thousands of years and can be found in many cultures. Although the word hypnosis is derived from the Ancient Greek word for sleep, hypnosis is not about being unconscious. Instead, the client is placed in an altered state of focused attention. In this state, he or she becomes more suggestible. It feels a lot like that time when you are just about to fall asleep, and you are totally relaxed (Elman, 1964).

Hypnosis works by the power of suggestion. If you believe you will be healed, then you will be. Scientists call this the placebo effect. There is some evidence that hypnosis was used by the ancients in Egypt, Greece and Rome. The temple of Imhotep in Saqqara was an important healing centre in 300 BCE. Clients would eat herbs, and there would be hours of recitation of prayers. Then the client was guided to a dark chamber to sleep and wait for a dream which would suggest a cure. Shamans in indigenous cultures also spent time in trance states which are just like hypnotic experiences. These experiences can be traced back thousands of years to the earliest days of human life (Shamanicjourney.com, 2023).

In more recent times, hypnosis was developed by Franz Mesmer, who lived in the 1700s. He applied magnets to his clients' bodies, often causing them to fall down into trance states and effecting miraculous cures. Hypnosis was further developed scientifically by James Braid, an English surgeon in the 1800s. He could perform medical operations on patients without anaesthetic using the powers of the mind. Hypnosis was also used as a tool by the great psychologist Sigmund Freud. He placed his clients in a trance to allow them the freedom to talk about anything without inhibition. He gave up using hypnosis as a method as he feared it was encouraging his clients to fall in love with him. He began to use free association instead, where clients just laid on his couch and talked about whatever came into their heads. In the 1950s, there was an explosion of scientific research into hypnosis, and Milton Erickson remains one of the best-known hypnotherapists of this period. Erickson became famous for being able to cure people of all kinds of mental distress (Elman, 1964).

Today, the reputation of hypnosis is somewhat tarnished. Many people associate it with the entertainment of stage hypnotists, which means lots of people do not take it seriously. Also, people worry they will be brainwashed or fall under the spell of the hypnotist. None of this is true. You don't do anything in hypnosis that you don't want to do. In England, where I live, hypnotherapy is not usually available from the National Health Service as it is regarded not to have a strong enough evidence base. In spite of this negativity, I have had great success with some clients. Sadly, there do seem to be some unprofessional hypnotherapists and some who are more concerned about making money than helping people.

Studies have shown increased theta brain wave activity and hemispheric beta wave asymmetry when a client is in hypnosis. There are also changes in gamma oscillations. Interestingly, some people cannot be hypnotised, and brain scans show this brain wave activity is not occurring inside those people's minds. These individuals are only a small minority of the population (Jensen *et al.,* 2011). The therapist achieves this state of hypnosis by using soothing words to encourage the client to relax both their body and mind. It's all done with the voice, and there is no need for pendulums or watches or other gimmicks you might see in films. It's a lot like a deep meditation. While the client is totally relaxed, in the simplest form of hypnotherapy, the therapist makes suggestions about how to improve the client's life. For example, for weight loss, the therapist would make statements about eating less, eating healthy foods, exercising and so on. The suggestions go deep down into the client's subconscious mind and are accepted by the client. The therapist then counts the client back to full awareness. The person goes away and acts on the advice given without even realizing it. Clients just seem to naturally do what they have been advised to do. The session can be reinforced by a recording that the person listens to each day.

If the client finds that the suggestion therapy is not working, more can be done. The therapist can find the root cause of their issues by going back in time to find a reason for the unwanted behaviour. This is called regression therapy. Often, the cause will be found in childhood. It could be a memory that is almost forgotten. Perhaps a client is suffering from anxiety and doesn't know why. In a regression session, she might go back to an early memory of being lost in a shop. The child panicked as he or she could not find the parents and had feelings of abandonment and lack of safety. The subconscious mind has reacted to this situation by surmising that the world isn't safe. The primitive fight or flight mechanism is activated deep within the brain, and the client finds themselves easily anxious. To help the client, the therapist makes suggestions under hypnosis that the world is safe and all is well. The memory is cleared and released.

The client may have an ongoing problem that does not appear to have its root in childhood. Early pioneers of past-life regression therapy, like Michael Newton, discovered that they could take the client beyond childhood into a past life. Often, the root of the issue is found in this other life and is then released by the therapist and the client. I had a client who had unexplained weight gain. She was a super-healthy person. She ate vegan food and exercised daily. In spite of this, she could not get rid of her abdominal fat. Under hypnosis, she went back to a past life where she was starving and homeless on the streets of Victorian England. One day she just lay down in the street and died. I helped my client to clear this memory and gave her suggestions that there would always be enough food now, and she didn't need to worry about starving any more.

Hypnotherapy has been used successfully to heal a whole host of issues. Some clients can be healed in just one session, while others will need many more. It does not work for everyone. I've seen clients who seem to feel no effect whatsoever, whereas others change as if by magic overnight. Everyone is different.

Some researchers do not believe that the memories we have under hypnosis are real. There is a problem of bias that can creep into the process. The client may want to believe something has happened and so may the hypnotist. This desire for a certain outcome can unconsciously lead the client into certain memories. It is important not to lead the client with biased questions. Human memory is an extremely complicated process. The mind may fill in the gaps when some information is missing with events that did not actually happen. There have been cases of repressed sexual abuse memories that turned out to have been fabricated (Brent and Paterline, 2016). There is no way to prove scientifically that your memories under hypnosis are real. You must decide for yourself how they feel to you. It has been possible to verify some of the details that clients come up with in their past life sessions. Dr Weiss had a client called Catherine, who recalled several past lives in great detail. He was able to verify the information she gave him through public records and became convinced that it was true (Weiss, 1988). Some clients only receive vague impressions of their past lives, but others see vivid details and can see street signs and give exact dates. In the 1950s, there was the famous case of Bridey Murphy that caught the imagination of the public. Virginia Tighe, an American housewife, recalled amazing details about life in Ireland in the 1800s. As the case was so popular, investigative reporters checked out the details. For some, no evidence could be found though others were found to be true. The case is controversial to this day (Bernstein, 1956).

Michael Newton took the past life regression work even further and discovered he could take clients into what he called the place between lives. These kinds of sessions are called Life Between Lives sessions. It was this kind of session I had with Scott de Tamble. Firstly, the client is given a long, slow induction into a relaxed state. It is important to be deep in hypnosis for this purpose so that the conscious mind does not interfere with the memories.

Our rational mind is nothing but a hindrance here. It is constantly monitoring, adjusting and judging our thoughts and recollections. We want the client's spiritual side to run free without the constant reigning in of the logical brain. The mind can be thought of as made up of the conscious, the subconscious and the superconscious mind. The client moves between these layers during the session. We find that memories of past lives are stored in the subconscious while the superconscious holds our divine soul memories. In a Life Between Lives session, inductions consist of guided imagery to encourage the client to relax. The therapist can lead the client to travel down stairways, along paths, walk on beaches, meander through gardens or woodlands, hike through mountains or float in pools of water. These visualisations use all of the senses so that the client is totally immersed in the scene. Counting is also a way of deepening the hypnosis experience.

When the client is totally relaxed, the therapist guides the person back to a scene in childhood. Next, the therapist might suggest a particular age to go to and then ask the client to describe the front of their home and then to go inside and sense their bedroom. The hypnotist might ask the client to describe their favourite piece of clothing or a toy.

Then the therapist directs the client to an even earlier pleasant memory. It could be a birthday party or some other special day. Again, the therapist encourages the client to describe the scene in as much detail as possible.

After this, the therapist takes the client to the time of being inside the womb. The person might be able to describe a warm and dark place, and they may be able to hear their mother's heartbeat. The interviewer can ask the client at what month their soul joined the foetus and what they think of the circuitry of the baby's brain. Some souls come and go rather than staying with the growing baby. They can go to the spirit world, travel around and have all sorts of interesting experiences.

From the womb, the therapist takes the client into their most recent past life. Sometimes, other past lives are chosen. The hypnotist asks the client to visualise a long tunnel which takes them to their previous incarnation. The client can move through various times and scenes in this past life before being taken to the death scene. The person then moves away from the physical body into the spirit world. They feel no pain in the transition. The client may hover above the body for a while. The past life can be examined and discussed.

The therapist then guides the soul into the spirit world. There might be a guide here at the gateway to help the person on the way. It could be a deceased relative or a spiritual teacher. Often, clients will say they are in the midst of a great white light. As the client moves through the spirit world, they often become aware of lights in the distance. These are spiritual beings. The closest one is often the person's spirit guide. Sometimes, the guide appears to look like a human figure. The client may feel enveloped by a loving, healing energy. Often, the guide communicates with the person by telepathy – thoughts are placed in their mind, which they can tell the therapist.

The guide will then take the soul for orientation. The spiritual being heals the soul, who might experience being in a crystalline structure or being surrounded by walls of coloured light.

After healing, the client often finds themselves in a garden talking to their guide. Then, the past life is reviewed. The client thinks about what was positive about the life and also what was not achieved. Some clients then visit a library to learn something about themselves.

The next stop is visiting the soul group. The client meets their soul companions. These are like friends who travel through many lives with the client playing different roles. The client might meet them in open countryside or in temples. These soulmates could be spouses, friends or family members. The soul mates often appear as lights of different colours. It is also possible to meet a soul who is still incarnated on Earth. The reason is that souls do not bring all their energy to each life but leave a portion of it back home in the spirit world. You could think of this energy as the Higher Self.

After meeting the soul group, the therapist can take the client before The Spirit Council. Often the council will appear to be in some kind of temple. The client could have up to ten council members. The more members there are, the more advanced the soul is. The council members can appear as light forms or as humans, often dressed in elaborate robes. There can be a review of a past life and comments about soul advancement. The council members may wish to review several past lives. The client can also ask questions about their current life.

It is possible at this point for the client to be aware of some other presence presiding over everything, which can be thought of as God or source energy. This force is often more of a feeling than something the client sees directly.

Some clients will wish to visit other parts of the spirit world. There are spaces where souls are trained to use energy and uninhabited worlds where souls can practise energy manipulation. It is also possible to visit other dimensions where souls may study or play. Clients may visit a life selection room where souls can choose their next body. In addition, they may get advice from guides about their new life before they leave for their current life.

Finally, the client is gently taken out of hypnosis back to the present moment (Newton, 2004).

It was this kind of Life Between Lives session that I had. Mine did not follow the usual format at the insistence of my guides. They had lots of important things to tell me. Firstly, Scott gave me an induction to relax me and put my mind in the appropriate state of focused attention. I was guided to walk down a staircase. Each step was a year of my life. As I went down, I was becoming younger and younger. While my hypnotist was speaking, I was imagining an old stone folly in a wood, and the staircase was within this building. I could see everything vividly. The wood was filled with thousands of trees with full green leaves, and there were lots of woodland creatures scurrying around on the forest floor like rabbits, moles and mice. A great variety of birds were singing in the trees. The folly, in a clearing, was a tall tower of golden yellow stone. It had a pointed tiled roof with a weather vane on the top. The staircase was going down in a spiral, and I could see worn stone flags beneath my feet. There were little slits in the walls, which let some light in. I could see shafts of sunlight falling across the flagstones. The sense was of being inside a fairytale. It felt like I was a beautiful maiden off to have an adventure, finally escaping from the tower that had imprisoned me. I was excited as I ran down the steps because I felt I was going to have a wonderful experience.

I was then instructed to go back to some happy memories from childhood. I got off the staircase at the tenth step, so I was ten years old. I was guided to the house I had lived in as a child. I could see the green front door with a panel of bubbly glass in the top. There was a little front garden with flowerbeds around a neat rectangular lawn and a wrought iron gate. I noticed a small wall forming a barrier between the garden and the road. It was an ordinary brick-built semi-detached house built in the 1950s. There were lots of these across England, so there was nothing unusual about it. I went through the door and up the stairs to my childhood bedroom. I saw all my toys and my bed and the sliding wardrobe with my clothes in. I remember being particularly drawn to my toy gorilla called Jacko. He had rough brown fur and a rubber face. I particularly loved him because he had bendy arms that you could wrap around things. I then went to the wardrobe and picked out one of my favourite dresses. It was just a plain blue cotton dress, but I liked it. I didn't really have any fancy clothes at this time. I also noticed a vinyl record player that I use to play my ABBA records on. I remembered how lucky I was to have so many toys and books and a big room of my own to sleep in. I remembered I used to play schools with all my toys and line them up to play with in rows. I even made them little exercise books out of card and squared paper. I thought I might be a teacher one day. I loved my primary school and my teachers, as they were so kind to me. I believed that I was a good student.

I have mixed feelings about my childhood. Though I was a lot better off than most people on the planet, I always had a sense of not being quite at home with my family or amongst my peers. I felt different in a way I could never quite explain. In contrast to most of the children I knew, I was bookish and liked nothing better than reading in my bedroom. I felt calm when I was alone. I did have friends at this point, and we used to play together in the street and go down to the local stream that we called a beck. There was a rope slung across a tree so you could hold on and swing across the river. I used to go with some girls from my road. My best friend was Tracey. She was pretty with dark ringlets, and she also had beautiful dresses. She had a pony called Blaze. I was pretty jealous about this because we didn't have enough money for me to have a pony. I think my disappointment at this was the start of some of my psychological problems. Being poorer than others in our area made me feel different and somehow inadequate. Comparison is the thief of joy, as the saying goes. It was like I wasn't worthy enough to have something like that. I was completely pony mad at this point. I used to get all the horsey books out of the library and read them over and over again. It seemed that some children were having perfect lives riding across Exmoor on their horses with groups of friends and having adventures. I didn't understand why life had to be unfair like this. Some people got everything, and other people didn't even have enough to eat. I used to think about the children we used to learn about at school in faraway places who didn't have enough food or clothing. We used to donate to a charity in India called Goodwill Village. I felt so sorry for them and thought I should go and do that sort of work someday. I was definitely luckier than

them as I always had food to eat. Steak and chips on a Saturday was my favourite meal. It was a strange world I found myself living in with so much inequality.

I made my first attempts at manifesting a pony to no avail. I used to pray for one every night and write affirmations about it on anything I could find. It didn't work, though. I had a big lesson in not getting what I wanted. For some reason, the longing and yearning for something I couldn't have seemed to damage me. I think subconsciously; I interpreted it as a lack of love. I often felt that my parents didn't like me much. I felt I was a disappointment to them in some way. It was as if they wanted me to have a different personality and be a different person.

There was a lot of anger and bad temper in our house. It was all about how things looked on the surface. The illusion of a perfect family had to be kept up at all costs. My sister didn't bond with me either. We were never close, and she preferred her own friends. She was mean to me most of the time.

There were harsh words and harsh punishments. One example is I was kissing my dog on the rug in the living room. For doing this, my father kicked me and told me to go to bed even though it was early evening. To this day, I have no idea why I deserved such a punishment.

He was probably drunk, as he was quite often. I have a dog today that I kiss all the time, and I don't see anything wrong with it. Dogs love affection, and I love to give and receive kisses from them.

My sister was always fighting with me. She loved to cause me pain, and I always remember she used to make her lips go really thin as she hurt me. I sometimes think she was possessed by some kind of demon because of the way she behaved. There was a time she contracted scabies from someone at school. She had been told to keep away from me as it was so infectious. She deliberately came up to me in the living room and rubbed her hands all over me. So I got scabies too. I can never understand someone who behaves like this. It's deliberate meanness for no reason.

My mother could swing between being kind and unkind. She wanted everyone to think she was the perfect mother. When nobody was around, she was quite capable of saying nasty little comments. If ever I tried to praise myself, she would bring me down to size with a cutting remark. I was never allowed to think well of myself. I don't ever remember her saying that I was pretty or that she loved me. One of her favourite sayings was, "I want never gets." Apparently, it was wrong to want anything. People who thought well of themselves were disparaged as 'I love me' types. When I was going through puberty, I was often sweaty and had greasy skin and spots, along with lots of other teenagers. Instead of being sympathetic, she would comment that *her* skin had been perfect at my age. Also, she didn't tell me anything about periods or sex. I had to find out from friends. When I became an adult, she was always telling me that I was fat. I didn't realise how unhealthy my family's behaviour was until I was much older.

I studied Psychology and learned about scapegoating. I think I was the scapegoat of my family. In ancient times in Israel, a goat would be chosen to take on all the sins of the village. The people would beat the goat and drive it out of the community so they could feel their sins had been absolved. This term is now used to describe a member of a dysfunctional family who is blamed for everything (Allport, 1954). For some reason, I was the one that nobody liked. In spite of the harsh words of my childhood, I think this way of behaving with children was quite common and probably still is. Parents carry their own unresolved trauma from their own childhoods and pass it on to their children. They just don't know how to parent properly. I know a lot of people had childhoods much worse than mine, with beatings, sexual abuse and extreme poverty. I hope this book can help others to heal like I did.

The British class system I live in is brutal, and if you feel at the bottom of it as I did, you can feel inadequate all your life. In England, there is great prejudice about people from the north as I am. People laugh at our accents and seem to think we are all stupid. Industrial places are often looked down on as ugly and working class. Lots of people are obsessed with social status and money. It's a deeply sick society and does not seem to be getting any better.

Anyway, back to my session, we go.

Then, Scott instructed me to leave that scene and go back to the staircase. Down and down I went. This time I got off at the sixth step. It was Easter, and my family were on a day trip to Whitby, a pretty seaside town on the Yorkshire coast. I was wearing a white crocheted dress with a pink ribbon. We were all wearing our best clothes as it was a special occasion. I was eating a chocolate egg. It was a cold, windy day but sunny. I could smell the sea and hear the seagulls whirling around in the sky. We were standing in front of Whitby Abbey, which is a ruin on a hill overlooking the town. There was my Mum and Dad, my sister and my Gran. I remember I used to love our day trips out and about. These kind of days were my favourite memories of my childhood. I enjoyed pottering around new places. The sea and the moors of Yorkshire were so beautiful. The northern moors were always full of sheep who wandered around everywhere as there were no fences. They were often on the road blocking your way. I loved to see them so much, especially in the spring when they had their lambs. There was a sense of space where you could feel free. I often wished I could live in the countryside instead of the town. The sea also amazed me. It was always freezing cold, but sometimes, in the summer, we went in for a dip. I loved the salty air and the sound of the birds. The sea seemed so powerful, yet the wave sounds were calming. There was a freshness about sea air that made me feel good.

CHAPTER TWO:

The Womb

After that, I went back to the staircase and continued down to 0. When I left the last step; I was in the womb. I remember it was dark and warm. It felt roomy and comfortable. I was aware that my mother was feeling anxious, and I didn't know why. It made me worry about being born as I felt that something was wrong. I think my mother was always an anxious person though she would never admit it. I have inherited this tendency to anxiety.

She came from an extremely poor family, as her parents had thirteen children. I imagined she was pretty pleased to get married and have her own home. All the family stories seemed to be about poverty and suffering. I remember she used to have to take time off school to help her mother with the washing. All the girls seemed to have to do a lot of the tasks around the house and look after the younger siblings. I think sometimes they didn't even have enough to eat. There are small black-and-white photos of them wearing big boots with no socks. My mother's family lived in an old shop in the dock part of town. This area had always had a bad reputation and was referred to ominously as 'over the border'. I think this kind of childhood would damage a person, whoever they were. I sensed that my mother was disappointed with life. I was to be the second child as she already had a daughter.

The stories on my father's side were no better. He had five brothers and sisters and had grown up in a council house in Dundee. The house had been put up hurriedly after the war, and the top half was made of metal. When we visited my Gran, it was absolutely freezing in winter. His father had been a Steeple Jack and in the merchant navy but seemed to spend a lot of time in the pub drinking. He died young, when my father was sixteen. There were stories of not having shoes to wear, so they cut down Wellington boots. My father had come down to Middlesbrough to find work at sixteen and married my mother young. He took after his father as he drank a lot and was often out in the pub with his friends. He had a vile temper. I'm not sure why he wanted children, as he didn't seem to enjoy spending any time with me. I have to forgive my parents for their inability to love me, as I don't think they knew any better. They had both grown up in harsh environments.

I was born at home in a terraced house overlooking the steelworks in the industrial town of Middlesbrough. It was a humble beginning. I can't remember the house very well as we moved away from it when I was three. I had a feeling of black soot everywhere and polluted air. The steelworks made noise all day and all night, clanging and banging of metal on metal, fires and smoke and black filth. It was Mordor.

I think part of my anxiety in the womb was the worry that my parents had wanted a boy. I could hear them discussing how great it would be if they had a son. They even had a name ready for me: Sean. They then would have the perfect family of one girl and one boy, just like my mum's sister. As a baby in the womb, hearing this, it was no wonder that I felt trepidation about my new life. I was seriously considering giving up the idea and going back to the spirit world. When it came to my birth, I was actually a breach. I wonder if this was my attempt not to come out. It was a difficult birth, and my mother must have had a lot of pain. The midwife helpfully said that babies usually die when they are born breached. How charming!

Apparently, when I was born, I was blue all over, and the doctor told my mother that nobody was to touch me. Eventually, the blue wore off, and I had normal skin. To this day, I have no idea what that was. Even today, I don't like strange people touching me. I tend to flinch away.

I know these birth details from my mother telling me. We didn't go through the birth in the Life Between Lives session. It seemed I had had a difficult beginning.

Back to the womb. I could feel that my mother was always busy. She was doing housework and painting a door. She didn't like to rest or take it easy. Then, Scott asked me when my soul energy joined the baby. I realised I was saying: 'They said' and I was talking about some other energies. They said my soul entered in the sixth month. So before this, the growing baby did not have the soul present. I think this probably has interesting applications for laws about abortion. It seems that the soul can enter the body whenever it wants and can also come and go. Typically, the soul does not enter at conception but waits awhile. These spirit energies were pleased with my intelligence and my potential. Also, they had given me more of the 'spirit'. They made sure I had a connection to them and asked me not to forget them. I learned I had chosen a difficult life deliberately though I knew it was going to be hard. I was aware at this point that I had struggled with emotions for a great deal of my life, and I had issues with depression and anxiety. These feelings made me start to become upset, and I could feel my voice cracking. They told me I must never forget the light. I was a different kind of being, so I was going to find this life difficult. The others told me I was not the same as other humans. People were of a more primitive race than mine. I described human beings as very low. I said they were like insects grubbing around in the dirt, and I couldn't understand them or why they behaved as they did. I am ashamed to admit this is what I said, but I did. I just didn't get people. I have found they are not usually interested in the same things as me but are stuck on seeking pleasure and diversion. They identify with their bodies rather than their souls and have no desire to develop their spirituality. Of course, this does not apply to everyone, but the people I met seemed to be like this.

I was an extremely shy child, and nowadays, I would have been diagnosed with anxiety. I was afraid of people and of some things in the world. I didn't speak much. There were two golden retriever dogs two doors down, but whenever I saw them in the alleyway, I just went back into the house. My fear of dogs was completely irrational as I had never been attacked by them. I also remember feeling depressed from an early age. It was as if I just didn't want to be on Earth, and I didn't know what I was doing with this family in this place. I used to cry at night a lot, and I wet the bed until I was ten. Truly, I was a troubled child. I remember having terrible nightmares where people were trying to attack me. They appeared to be dressed like pirates, and they were trying to stab me through the mattress or hurt me in other ways. I used to have a recurring dream where I could see myself in some kind of mortuary. I was lying down, looking down at my legs which were aching. I was wearing a kind of tunic, but most of my legs were bare. The place had an evil, creepy atmosphere. I would often sleepwalk and wake up screaming.

Then, at this point in the womb experience, Scott asked to speak to these other beings who were talking to me directly.

CHAPTER THREE:

Malalia – The First Spirit Guide

I was aware that someone else's voice was speaking through me. She said, 'I am Malalia. I am from the stars. I'm from there.' As she was speaking, I was aware of her in my mind's eye. She appeared as a beautiful tall woman wearing a white robe that covered her body right up to the neck. She had blonde hair swept up in a French roll. Malalia was extremely old in appearance but still strikingly attractive. There were lots of similar beings standing behind her, and they were all dressed in a similar way. Some were male, and some were female. Malalia reminded me of an angel though she didn't have any wings that I could see. She seemed to have a high vibrational energy and a calm wisdom about her. I had the feeling she was thousands of years old and extremely knowledgeable about spiritual matters. She was definitely a high being.

Malaysia told me my soul's name was Kokua. I struggled to say it as if the word was from a different language. I had never heard of this name, but when I researched it later, I found it was Hawaiian and meant a spirit of kindness and helping other people without expecting anything in return. I am proud to bear such a name for my Higher Self. In Hawaii, people help each other out and have a great sense of community. It's about being selfless and thinking of others (Shelivesaloah.com, 2023). I think where I live, we have lost this in recent years, and everyone seems to be living in a selfish bubble. I wish we could achieve a greater sense of community. Some people do it, but most don't seem interested. I have always tried to be kind and to help others though I have not always been successful. If we could all try to activate the spirit of Kokua within us, everything would be so much better.

The aliens had sent me to Earth to have an experience and come back better. When asked about the homeworld, Malalia said it was far away, and we didn't know it. When pressed, she said we would call it Venus, but that wasn't what they called it. It was a spiritual world rather than a physical one. I think the guides were trying to explain it in a different dimension. They said, 'You have to go somewhere else to get there'. When I later asked my guides how to say Venus in their language, the reply was a series of clicks and sounds that were impossible to reproduce.

Malalia explained my purpose on Earth was to raise the vibration and bring the light. I wasn't sure how I was supposed to do this. As I was explaining to my therapist what was being communicated, the spiritual beings were also putting images in my head and speaking with me telepathically. It was like words were not necessary. I just needed a speech to explain to Scott what was going on. Malalia put an image of the Queen of Dragons from the TV series Game of Thrones (hbo.com, 2023) in my head: Daenerys Targaryen. She was standing on a platform addressing her massed troops and exhorting them to fight. I had always admired her beauty and strength when I watched the show. I didn't feel I was capable of leading an army like she did. I have always been shy and tended to work in the background. I enjoyed the show Game of Thrones to a point, but I found it too violent for me, and I stopped watching it. I've never been good around violence. I think Malalia was instilling confidence and self-belief in me. These qualities are ones I have been working on as I have always felt I lacked confidence in my own ability. She told me there is spiritual warfare going on in the spiritual world, and my guides and I are on the side of the light. We need to fight the forces of darkness that are very real. I have found that many people in the spiritual community try to deny the darkness. They want to believe everything is love and light. We only have to look around the world to realize that there are dark forces at work. It's as if the evil exists within people.

They can choose light, or they can choose darkness. Michael Newton did not seem to believe in evil entities or what you might call demons. In contrast to this view, my guides appear to be saying that there are entities with evil intentions. It's as if the Star Wars movies (Starwars.com, 2023) or the Star Trek TV series (Startrek.com, 2023) were actually right. In the Star Wars film, there is an evil empire called the Imperial Forces under a dark entity called Darth Vader. Luke Skywalker heroically rescues the kidnapped prisoner and defeats the power of the darkness. In Star Trek, there is an intrepid group of military astronauts who man a spaceship through the galaxy. They belong to the United Federation of Planets. The personnel consists of a mixture of humans and aliens who are benevolent and try to solve the problems they encounter on various planets. Again, the crew often encounter evil alien beings who are making war in the universe.

My guides suggested that there are good aliens and evil aliens who are having some kind of cosmic battle. It seems that these two forces are also involved in influencing events on Earth. I am on the side of the Light, as are all the Venusians. The battle between good and evil is also being mirrored in the hearts of human beings. The Venusians want people to turn towards the Light so that they do not destroy themselves or the Earth. We are all aware that we seem to be on the edge of ecological catastrophe due to human greed. We also seem to be close to nuclear war at times. We must not give in to the darkness within ourselves.

It was interesting to me that Daenerys looked like a younger version of Malalia. Part of my mission is to lead a spiritual army back to the light to save the Earth from the evil that currently encapsulates it. I am doing this metaphorically through this book. I am not sure how to do it in a more real-world sense. I suppose if I could persuade enough people to awaken to the spiritual truth, we could become a spiritual army and help the Earth and the souls living on it. It seems like there are benevolent aliens like the Venusians but some that do not have good intentions. The evil aliens seem to have control of some institutions on Earth, and some parts of our planet have been made dark by them. They do their work by influencing the minds of human beings. The angels talked to me in terms of dark and light all the time. They meant this in a spiritual sense. Darkness has nothing to do with skin tone but is about the evil inside people's hearts. I hope as you read this book, you will want to join me in the Army of Light. It seems that we do not have to wait for Heaven, but we can have Heaven on Earth now if enough of us look within to awaken. Peace and love are deep inside of us, and we can access this wonderful feeling through meditation. Everyone has the ability to communicate with their spirit guides. Awakening means knowing the reality of the spiritual world which is all around us. Then we must tell others this good news.

In later meditations, the spirit guides showed me visions of Kokua fighting dark forces. The demons, if that is what they are, looked like snakes or sea creatures with lots of legs and tentacles. I was fighting them with a sword. I was also shown a place full of strange creatures that seemed to be spewing some horrible substance from their mouths like they were being sick. My Higher Self fights for the light in the spiritual realms against the forces of evil. I think these images were metaphorical to show me that the Light is struggling to win.

So raising the vibration seems to need some explanation. Spiritual beings vibrate at a much higher or faster rate than human beings. It's a big effort for spirits to speak to us as they have to lower their vibration to meet ours. We can raise our vibration through love. You can think of your vibration as like a ceiling fan that goes round and round. You can increase the vibration to make it spin faster. The faster it spins, the harder it is to see. Giving love in the sense of compassion to others increases our rate. We can then rise up and find it easier to communicate with our spiritual guides or angels. To rise, you need to keep loving kindness at the forefront of your mind at all times. This is a concept in Buddhism and Christianity. If you open your heart, the spirit world can come through. You can't just love your immediate friends and family. The kindness needs to extend to all of humanity, even your enemies. You can begin by picturing someone you love very much. Just hold the person in your mind's eye and pour all your love from your heart into them. I started with my dog as I found it so hard to do this love meditation with people. When you become better at this exercise, you can extend your love to people you don't like or to whole nations.

Gratitude is another brilliant way to raise your vibration. There is always something to be thankful for. When your wake up in the morning, you can give thanks for being alive. Then you can thank God for the bed you have slept in. You can be thankful for having eyes to see the world. Whatever your situation, start up a daily gratitude practice and watch your life improve. When you feel sad or angry, just think of something to be grateful for. Have you ever noticed when you are visiting developing countries, lots of people seem to be really happy even though they have so little? I remember once I was holidaying in the hills of Morocco, and as I was hiking along, I came across a group of little boys diving into a lake. They were having an incredible amount of fun, laughing and shrieking with joy, and yet they were from poor rural families. They knew how to make the best of their environment.

Another method of raising your vibration is to live in a spirit of generosity. Give freely to others with what you have. If you feel you don't have enough money, you can give a little to a charity. If you feel lonely, then reach out to others with a smile. You can also be generous with your time by volunteering. Helping others makes you feel better inside yourself. There is an old saying that it is better to give than receive, and it is actually true. Just try it.

Meditation is another way of raising your vibration. Start a simple practice every day. Sit comfortably and focus on your breathing. Allow thoughts to come and go and stay in the present moment. Breathwork during meditation will help you even more. Breathe in and out through the nose as deeply as you can. Then you can experiment with breathing through alternate nostrils, covering the other with your finger. A meditation or yoga teacher can help you with your practice.

Forgiveness is key to living in a high vibration. Blaming others weighs down your energy and stops you from progressing. Forgiving people does not mean that you condone their behaviour. You are forgiving others for yourself, not for them. Just hold your enemy in your mind's eye and tell them that you forgive them. If you don't feel different at first, just keep saying it until you do. You can release all your heaviness and feel full of light.

Physically you can raise your vibration by eating healthy foods. Organic fruit and vegetables will help. Try to source them locally and eat them fresh just as they are. Their vibration will pass along to you. This is not so easy in England in the winter. I can become tired of carrots. Avoid frying, too much meat and processed foods. Think like an ancient forager, and you will be on the right track. Give up alcohol and drugs. You know you are taking these substances to numb the pain of living in this world. Try to embrace life without crutches. Feel all your feelings fully and release them. Your vibe should rise as a result.

Next, you can try paying attention to your thoughts. Change pessimistic or anxious thoughts to more positive ones. It's hard at first, but you can feel improvement with time. Always speak kindly about yourself. Forgive yourself for your mistakes and move forward.

Be careful what you give your attention to. We are surrounded by negative information. I find I have to avoid a lot of news these days. The media are constantly telling us to be terrified. Currently, there is an awful war going on in Europe which could escalate at any moment. We are also told there is an imminent climate catastrophe in progress that could destroy the Earth. I limit my intake to a little each day. We have to be informed to some extent, but the barrage of negative information is too much to take. It's similar to our entertainment, such as films and TV shows. Try to seek out ones with an upbeat message rather than all the violence and horror they serve up. Books are great, so seek ones that can help your spiritual development. Music can also be so helpful if it is uplifting.

We can also raise our vibration by surrounding ourselves with beauty. Prettify your home with objects that are pleasing to you. Pay attention to colour schemes that you find inspiring. The tiniest change can make a difference. Get rid of things that don't serve you – release the clutter. Spend as much time as you are able in the beauty of nature. It will lift you into the light.

Surround yourself with people that make you feel good. You need friends that are positive about you and see the good in you. There are good people in the world, so you just need to find them. Find groups where people are on the same spiritual path as you. You can help to keep each other in a high vibrational state. A sense of community is such a powerful thing if we can achieve it. I think community is something that has been lacking in my country of late. In the village where I currently live there isn't much of a centre. It's just houses with no facilities. Even the church is badly attended, so there is not much coming together there either. We have occasional village events, but day to day; most people are hidden in their houses. I interact with dog walkers as I meet them, but we don't go much beyond surface pleasantries for a few minutes. Some residents of the village are actively unfriendly and don't attend any of the occasional activities. It is such a shame, but it seems normal for many people in my country these days. I need to be the change though it's tough to figure out how. I would love to live in a genuine spiritual community where everyone co-operates and works together for the common good. It is possible if enough of us wake up.

I think the recent coronavirus scare, where we were locked down in our houses, was damaging to our spiritual development. We were kept separate from other people. Even a visit to the shops meant you had to stand several metres apart from other people. It is hard to show kindness and compassion under such circumstances. I felt the measures were draconian and an overreaction. I think this is an example of dark forces being in charge of the world. It seemed like there was an anti-people agenda. The forces in charge of the planet wanted us fearful, obedient and not in communication with others. This is against a spiritual view of the world. Sadly, most people were beaten down to compliance. There was a loss of freedom. Is there some dark purpose at work here that we are not seeing clearly?

I am fully aware that none of this spiritual behaviour is easy. Many of us are struggling with unfulfilling work and poverty. We may be trapped in abusive relationships or living in concrete jungles. Just focus on one step at a time. Do the smallest of things to raise your vibration each day. I am still working on this myself, and I often have bad days. I feel like the Earth is always trying to drag me down, and I have to focus on rising up all the time.

I have spent years of my life in a negative vibration. I remember as a teenager, I became part of the goth subculture, and this gave me the excuse to wallow in my negativity. Goths in my youth wore black all the time and listened to doomy music. We danced together in dark nightclubs and read each other Victorian poetry about death. Gothic novels were our staple fare. It seems ridiculous to me now that I embraced this movement so wholeheartedly when it obviously was not going to do me any good mentally. I think now I understand it was a trauma response. We were growing up in dark times. In my youth, there was the constant threat of nuclear war, and the economy was in the process of being de-industrialized. There were few jobs, and our prospects were grim. Add to that it always seemed to be raining in Yorkshire, and you have the perfect environment in which goth culture could thrive.

Depression just came naturally to me. I have had to force myself to change and to be more positive. It is a daily struggle, and some days I feel low. Overall though, I have improved, and you can too.

It is important to accept yourself just as you are. As we are human, we all have light and darkness within us. Nobody is perfect. Accept your flaws and your past mistakes. Forgive yourself and move forwards. Self-love is the first step in being able to love others. It is hard for many of us. Write a love letter to yourself. Tell yourself everything that is good about you. Write affirmations about your good qualities down on Post-it notes and pin them all over the house. Don't compare yourself to others. Concentrate on your own journey. Before you were born, your soul agreed to come here for a special purpose. Your soul is learning and growing. You are a unique part of the whole, magical spiritual world. Inside you, there is a fractal of God. You are divine. You are special. You matter. You are significant.

Though it's not easy, it is imperative that we raise our vibration for the good of humanity. Each person can act as a beacon and lift others up around them. Together we can raise the frequency of the entire world. Raising our vibration helps us to keep in touch with the higher realms and receive spiritual wisdom. Let's all vibe high!

What does bring the light mean? The light is the term Malalia used for the spiritual world but particularly the forces of good within it. Bringing the light is telling people about the truth of the world beyond through talks or writing. Jesus is a familiar example to me of someone who did this through his teachings. Most people don't currently have a true picture of what the light is, as Jesus' words have been twisted over the centuries. When the Bible was put together in its final form, many people had axes to grind. Powerful people wanted to be in charge of the church, so they placed passages in the New Testament that suited their purposes. These were not the words of Jesus. One example is where Jesus says, 'I did not come to bring peace but the sword' (Matthew 10:34). This statement goes against everything that Jesus taught in other parts of the Bible. His message was one of love, not violence. The imagery of swords makes me think more of warring Roman Emperors rather than a simple man of God. The trouble we have now is we don't know what Jesus said and what he didn't. So how can we find out? Each person can have a discussion with Jesus or, indeed, any other spiritual master, such as Buddha, through meditation. Through direct contact, you can find true knowledge rather than through texts which have been twisted and changed. There are many ascended masters and guides who can tell you about the true light through direct contact in meditation. The focus is always on love.

I have discovered many lost books that have not been included in the Bible. There are so many, but some of the most famous are the Book of Enoch, the Gospel of Thomas, the Gospel of Peter, the Gospel of Mary Magdalene, and the Jubilees. Many of these texts were discovered as part of the Dead Sea Scrolls (Vermes, 2011), which were found at the Qumran Caves in Palestine in 1946 and in the following years. Other texts were found in what is known as the Nag Hammadi Library (Robinson, 2000), which was discovered in Egypt in 1945. Some of these gospels give a different picture of Jesus from the one we are familiar with from the New Testament. In the gospel of Mary Magdalene, we read that Mary was a favoured disciple of Jesus, and he shared information with her that was not given to the other followers of Jesus. Much of this was how to communicate directly with God. Sadly, much of the original manuscript is missing (Leloupe, 2002). In this gospel, Mary reminds us of the vastness of our potential. We can overcome ourselves until we become spiritual beings that are neither masculine nor feminine. The gospel of Mary matches what my angels tell me in meditation. The body is not important at death, but the soul goes on to Heaven. God does not have a gender but is referred to as 'the good'. There is no sin, and nobody goes to Hell. Salvation is achieved through inner transformation.

The Gospel of Philip tells us that Jesus often kissed Mary Magdalene on the lips (Antonov, 2008). It seems they had a special relationship. Only some of the early Church's writings about Jesus made it into what we now refer to as the Bible. These are the gospels of Matthew, Mark, Luke and John; the Acts of the Apostles; thirteen letters from Paul; the letter to the Hebrews; seven general letters and the Book of Revelation. This version of the New Testament was decided at the Council of Hippo in 393 CE and the Council of Carthage in 397 CE. These councils were attended by bishops, Roman Emperors and other important people of the time. They would have included gospels that suited their purposesI have always noticed how the roles of women are sidelined in the New Testament. They appear, but they are not referred to as disciples. In the apocryphal gospel of Mary Magdalene, we find Mary was the most favoured follower of Jesus, and she was teaching and debating along with the men. The misogyny of many men in the early Church has meant this information has been hidden. I have always been particularly disgusted by one of the letters from Paul that says women should be silent in the church (Corinthians 14:34). Why should they? These patriarchal attitudes say more about Paul's view of the world than any of the teachings of Jesus. It seems that some men just want power for themselves. We see misogyny even in the Church today, with the Roman Catholic Church not allowing women priests.

Jesus spent a lot of time teaching in parables or stories to help people understand his message. He was always reaching out to those on the margins of society – the lost sheep. I see a lot of supposed Christians today who are not following the way of Jesus. Some go to church each week but don't live a Christian life for the rest of the week, where they are focused on making money and not thinking of the less fortunate. Most people in my country don't even go to church at all but just focus on achieving material goods and following their bodily desires. It's certainly not easy to follow the way of life that Jesus set out, and I know I, for one, am failing most of the time. Imagine if more of us could try to do it with purity, though, rather than following dogma that does not have much to do with the teachings of Jesus.

So what would Jesus have us do? I asked him in channelling, and this is what he told me. Firstly, the name Jesus is an English version of his name. I have always called him Jesus, but it is not the name he prefers. His name at the time would have been Yeshua. This name is the Hebrew version of Joshua. He actually prefers Issie, which was his nickname. In the East, he is referred to as Issa. Yeshua does not want to be worshipped but is happy to be our friend.

He walks beside us rather than in front of us. He was human, just like we are, and understood us completely. Yeshua believes all people are equal. Anyone could do the things he did. He is not better than us and does not want to be elevated into a god-like being.

He was born into a poor Jewish family in Palestine at the time of the Roman Empire in the first century CE. His mother was called Mary, and she became pregnant as a young woman with Yeshua. He says his birth was not miraculous, and these details were added later in the Bible version. His father was a soldier in the Roman army of Greek origin. This is so amazing to me because once when I was on holiday in Greece, I saw a man beckoning people into a restaurant who looked exactly like Jesus appeared to me. When I see him in my mind's eye, he has long brown hair with a reddish tone mixed in. His eyes are brown, and he has a short, neat beard. He often appears in casual clothes like jeans and a denim shirt. He likes wearing sandals or going barefoot. He was the son of God in the sense that we are all sons of God. He was sent from God as a messenger and teacher to bring the light and show people how to live. He was special because he brought more of his spiritual energy to his incarnation on Earth. We all have Higher Souls where most of our energy stays in the spirit world, but we bring some of it to our Earthly lives. Jesus brought a lot of his energy to Earth with him, so he was more like a high spiritual being than a person. This is why he could manipulate energy so easily to heal the sick and perform miracles. We all have the capacity within us to do this if we learn how. Mary was not to blame for her pregnancy out of wedlock. She was actually raped. At that time, Roman soldiers had a lot of power and could do whatever they wanted in Israel. They took women as housemaids and concubines. Mary was treated in this way as she was so beautiful. Men desired her. When she became pregnant, the soldier threw her out.

Joseph agreed to marry her because he was a good man, and he knew Mary was a pious woman. His wife had died. They had other children together. At that time, it was not possible for a virtuous Jewish woman to live alone without a husband.

Yeshua had incarnated many times before and had evolved to a high level spiritually. After his birth, he was visited by Holy Men from the East. They were actually Buddhist monks from Tibet. They knew he was a great man as they had been watching the alignment of stars so they could tell when and where he was to be born. They thought he was a Buddha, as they would call it in their tradition, or a holy man. He was born in a stable in Bethlehem. His parents took him to Egypt because of the danger of King Herod finding him. Rumours had spread that a holy child had been born who would be a great king. Herod was worried about being overthrown and would have had him killed. Yeshua spent some years in Egypt, and then the family returned to Palestine when he was a small child. It was obvious that he was gifted from a young age. He learned all the Jewish lore and could quote passages from the Torah.

He loved to debate spiritual matters. His gifts attracted attention in the little town of Nazareth where they lived. Joseph taught Yeshua carpentry, and they worked together in the little house in the town. His parents, realizing how special he was, let him go to school with the Essenes. The Essenes were a spiritual community who lived in a compound on the banks of the Dead Sea. They were spiritual and wore white clothing. They bathed in water each day and had great knowledge of all kinds of things. Yeshua went to school there with John the Baptist.

They were vegetarian, and some of them practised celibacy. They lived communally and shared the daily tasks. They had no money. They prayed together and believed in compassion for the poor. Anger was frowned upon in their community. The Essenes had their own secret sacred writings, which they taught to Yeshua. He loved to learn and enjoyed his time with them.

When Yeshua was thirteen, he was considered to be a man in the Jewish culture, and he had his Bar Mitzvah and was dedicated to God in the temple in Jerusalem. Even at this age, he was arguing with the Jewish priests about interpretations of scripture, and he spoke with great knowledge and eloquence. His parents wanted

Yeshua to get married and continue with the family business of carpentry. Issie was strong-willed, and he had other ideas. He had a rich uncle called Joseph of Arimathea who had business interests all over the world. Yeshua went with him on ships to various destinations. He even went to Cornwall and Glastonbury in England. Yeshua had a yearning for travel and spiritual knowledge, so he wanted to go East and learn about the beliefs of the Orient. At the time, the Silk Road was busy with merchants going back and forward from Israel to India and China. Yeshua joined a camel train and set off exploring.

Yeshua passed through Persia, where he met followers of the Zoroastrian faith. This belief system has a lot in common with Issie's faith. The Zoroastrians believe in a supreme creator God who is all-good. There are forces of chaos opposing God in the human world. A pantheon of lesser gods is a feature of the religion. It is important to have good thoughts, good words and good deeds. Issie argued with the priests about spirituality and taught people his own ideas. This behaviour angered the leaders, and they threw Yeshua out of the city and left him lying in the road.

Yeshua went on with his travels and entered India. Here he lived and studied with the Hindu Brahmins. Again, he argued with the priests, and he was in trouble for teaching the poor and lowly. The Brahmins believed that the lowest caste were not worthy of knowing the spiritual teachings, but Yeshua taught them everything he knew. The ordinary people loved him, but he was in fear of his life because of his views, so he went high up into the Himalayas. Though Hinduism appears to have a supreme creator, the Hindus do worship a whole host of gods and have idols in their temples. Yeshua disapproves of this. He also believes all people are equal and all can come to the light.

Yeshua actually went into what was then called Tibet but is now part of India, and he learned many things about spirituality in the monastery at Hemis. He became adept at manipulating energy and could do amazing things. Elderly monks taught him these things, and he read a lot of spiritual books that they had in the monastery. He spent a lot of time praying and meditating, so he received spiritual messages to help him from God. He also travelled to other monasteries in the Himalayas. Yeshua learned yoga and many forms of meditation. One of the most significant meditations is called The Rainbow Body. In deep meditation, it is possible to learn how to transform the body into five radiant lights. These lights are like the colours of the rainbow. It is as if the material body is transcended. It is also possible to slow down the heart rate so that the meditator appears almost dead. It was in these monasteries that he learned how to levitate, to walk on water and to heal the sick with energy from his hands. As Yeshua had brought nearly all of his Higher Self's spiritual energy to Earth, all of these

The Light Book

things were easy for him to achieve. These special yogas took ordinary monks decades to perfect, and many would never achieve them.

Travelling long distances was easy for Issie this time. He often just walked. There were places to stay along the Silk Road specially set up for travellers. He didn't need money as he could barter for his food and lodging. Issie was good with his hands, and he could repair roofs and wooden structures. He also healed people in exchange for what he needed.

Yeshua returned to Israel when he was twenty-nine. He had a broad experience of many things. He told people about what he called The Way, which is how he wanted them to live. He had innate knowledge direct from God, and he synthesized this with what resonated for him in the different religions he had studied. He was already confident in preaching to crowds. It was wonderful for him to be reunited with his family and old friends. They travelled all over Palestine preaching to the poor. He attracted many followers who were both men and women.

Here is what Jesus taught. We should love God. This does not mean we need to worship in a church or a temple. We can have a direct relationship with God through meditation and prayer. God is not an old man on a cloud. This image is a false light. God can be thought of as the unity of all things. He is in everything: every rock, every stone, in water, fish, birds and animals. He is in you and me. God is not male but rather embodies both male and female aspects. The energy of God is in the world we see around us but also in the spirit world. God resides there as well as in the world. The true nature of God is beyond time and space. It is not possible to comprehend God with the human mind. In this world, which we might call Heaven, all things are possible. It is a place full of love. We incarnate on Earth from there but forget all about it as we are born. Our task is to remember by meditating and praying. We can then remember our true nature as spiritual beings. We become aware of our eternal souls within us. Through going within, we can join back with God. We can all become One. This is how we achieve Heaven on Earth. Our lives on Earth are an opportunity for our souls to learn and grow. Our souls are eternal, and we all have many incarnations.

As well as loving God, we must love ourselves and each other. We do this by showing kindness and compassion to everybody. Open your heart to all beings. Being loving raises our vibration so we can go back to the light. God will provide us with everything we need here on Earth if we have faith in Him. Loving others and forgiving them for what they have done to us helps us to get off the wheel of karma and dwell in bliss. We must stay in the light and not do bad things. Jesus is the bridge between us and God. All our wrongdoings have already been forgiven. We have nothing to fear. We are not going to Hell. We just need to love. There is no sin in the ultimate reality. It is an illusion, so there is nothing to forgive. Yeshua has already provided atonement. We can join with God. There is no need for separation.

Our spirituality can be deeply personal. We do not need to talk to God in the formal way that most Churches suggest. There is no need for any kind of sacrifice to God, neither human nor animal. Through meditation and prayer, we can gain spiritual power. We can learn to heal others and to perform miracles. It is just a matter of having enough faith. We must tell others about the real message of Jesus – spread the light.

When we die, we all go to the same place. You might call it Heaven. Only your soul goes here, not your body. It does not matter what happens to your dead body on Earth. You don't need it. God does not judge you, but you judge yourself by reviewing your life. You see your good and bad actions. With your angels or guides, you can see what you could have done better. After a time, you may choose to incarnate again to benefit your soul journey. You will learn more lessons and try to do better in your life. The ultimate aim is to perfect your soul so that you can stay permanently in Heaven with God.

Yeshua taught all of these things to the common people of Israel. He began to attract the attention of the Romans, who thought he was a threat to their power. In fact, Issie had no desire for political strength. He was only concerned with the inner spiritual life. It was actually the Romans who had Jesus crucified, not the Jewish leaders, as it says in the Bible.

Issie was tortured in prison. He was beaten and severely whipped. He had to carry the crossbar of the cross to the place of his execution. He was so exhausted from the beatings he could

barely walk. He was placed on the cross and suffered the agonies of crucifixion for many hours. There were Roman soldiers who were secret followers of Jesus. With the help of these men and through the use of bribes, Joseph of Arimathea managed to have Yeshua taken down from the cross earlier than would have been usual. He took him away to a cave. Issie was not actually dead at this point. He used his Tibetan yoga techniques to relieve his pain and to slow his breathing. He managed to enable his spirit to leave his body temporarily.

Issie's body was laid in the tomb wrapped in a shroud, but Joseph bribed the guards and took his body to a secret location. Here he was tended to by his mother, Mary, and other devoted followers. Issie's spirit returned to his body. Using herbs and ointments like myrrh Yeshua's wounds were healed. He was given soup and soft foods. His strength returned, and he could walk again. He was alive, but he had to use a secret identity to stay safe.

Buddhism has much wisdom within it, as do all other religions. It's like each religion has a little part of the truth but not the full picture. Jesus told me that all religions point to the same garden. Many of the teachings of Jesus sound like those of Buddhism. Yeshua tells us to love God and to love each other. This is just like the Buddhist idea of showing compassion to all beings. Buddhists also emphasize that life is full of suffering. The life of Jesus was filled with suffering as he knew he was going to be tortured and then suffer terribly on the cross. He relieved the suffering of others through his healing miracles. Buddhists are taught to think of the people of the world as their children and to relieve their suffering. Buddhism also puts a great deal of store in meditation. Jesus talks about praying a lot, but contemplative prayer is similar to meditating. He often goes off into a quiet place to pray in the Bible. He is meditating at these points. Jesus does not advocate violence, as we see in his famous exhortation to turn the other cheek when you are wronged (Matthew 5:38). Buddhists also follow a non-violent path. Greed is frowned upon in Buddhism, and Jesus also often spoke against riches. When a rich man who is pious and living a good life asks Jesus what he should do to be better, Jesus tells him to sell all his possessions and follow him (Matthew 19:21).

However, Buddhism seems to differ from Christianity as it does not have an idea of an all-powerful deity. There are so many different religions with various beliefs and practices it is tricky to know which way to turn. The answer is to go deep within your own mind and find out the truth for yourself. A daily practice of meditation will gradually bring you into contact with the divinity inside you. You can then start to have spiritual experiences which will bring you wisdom (Dalai Llama, 2019).

Malalia told me I am supposed to write all kinds of books on spiritual topics, both fiction and non-fiction. I need to tell people about the light. I must listen to Malalia and keep my connection with the spiritual world. Her words were: let go, be free, trust. I have to release my sadness and rise up and be lighter. I am trying to do this through this book you are reading now.

So what did Malalia mean by letting go? Letting go in a spiritual context reminds me of the Buddhist concept of detachment. We are to detach from the material world. It is the spiritual life that is important, not the world we see around us. So we can stop trying to control everything and let outcomes flow naturally. We can surrender our desires. In our human bodies, we have an ego which is trying to run the show. Our ego is concerned with all the matters of the body. It is seeking comfort and material wealth. As we look around today, we can see our whole society seems to be built on this concept. Everyone is striving to be rich and famous, it seems. This kind of behaviour is not a spiritual impulse. We can trust in God to know what is best for us. If we can let go, our suffering will cease. I have suffered by being too attached to the outcome I wanted. All it brought me was pain. Letting go can bring us joy and love. It's not easy to do, and I struggle with letting go daily.

Malalia also told me to be free. It is incredibly difficult to be free in our society. We are told to work all day, buy a house at vast expense and spend all our money on taxes, food and paying bills. For most people, it is not a free existence. I often think of the wandering Sadhus you see in India, who seem to be some of the few people who have achieved freedom. These holy men have dedicated their lives to achieving enlightenment. They have no possessions and live by begging. (Klostermaier, 2007). I am not sure how to be free, but this is a concept I am pondering. Freeing myself from material desires is one step towards it.

Malalia also told me to trust the angels and guides. We all need to trust that there is a plan we are all a part of. It is hard to see this plan from our human perspective, and it does not make sense to us now. Trusting completely is hard for me. I tend to be a natural worrier, so trusting is something to work on. I tend to think that I can't take risks as I might end up homeless on the street without any food to eat. I know such thinking is preventing me from fully fulfilling my purpose, so I must learn to trust. By trusting, we open to our true potential. Trusting entails living in the present moment.

Scott asked the cause of my sadness, and Malalia said it was because there was no real love on Earth. This lack causes me sadness. It is true that I don't feel loved. I didn't feel loved as a child, and I don't feel loved now. People have said they loved me, but I don't feel it. It's as if Earth people cannot love in the same way that Venusians do, and I miss it. My attempts to gain love for myself have always seemed to end badly or be troubled. It's like I have so much love to give, but nobody even wants it. I find romantic relationships and even friendships are fraught with difficulties. My response in recent years has been to withdraw and spend a lot of time alone. I seem to give too much and not receive the same in return. I have found human love often seems transactional. People are giving in the expectation of receiving something in return. They do not love for the sake of love. As a young person, I loved the idea of romantic love we see in books and films where people are consumed with passion. They are willing to give up everything for the one they love. I found that real relationships fall far short of this ideal. Real love is not really romantic love which is more linked to sexual chemistry than compassion for others. The pursuit of romance led me into a lot of pain.

My only true love relationships have been with animals. I have an incredible love for my dog, and he returns this love. My dog Didi is often the only thing keeping me going in life. He is from Romania, and he was a homeless street dog. He was found after being run over by a truck, so he only has the use of three legs. I also used to have a cat called Willow, who I loved immensely. I also rescued another cat called Monty. One of my happiest childhood memories is riding an ex-racehorse called Lola along a beach in Yorkshire. Also, I had a dog called Sandy as a child who was capable of great love. I loved horses. Horses seemed to be from another world too. I had a bond with them. Nothing beats the freedom of galloping along on a horse. I think animals seem capable of giving unconditional love in a way that human beings cannot do. Your dog doesn't care if you haven't brushed your hair or you've gained a few pounds. They love you anyway.

When I was young, my dating experiences were usually disastrous. I found that a lot of men are only interested in what you look like. Their interest in you is sexual. They don't care for your conversation or your opinions. This is not the love that I am seeking. Then you have friends and acquaintances who only like you if you agree with them on all topics and accompany them to do the things that they want to do. If you don't conform to what they want you to be, you are dropped. I know there are good, loving people in the world, but they seem to be few in number. I spent a lot of time attracting the wrong sort. I mistook love for romantic love, but I have found the kind of love in books and films does not seem to be common. It's probably not even beneficial. A real connection between two souls is a rare thing indeed.

Many people love their parents, but I haven't been able to manage this. I didn't bond well with my mother or my father. We had nothing in common, and I felt they were harsh in discipline and not warm or compassionate. I think this kind of strict upbringing was common in England among my generation. We were distant and cold with each other. My sister bullied me throughout my childhood, and to this day, I feel nothing for her. I have realized that I have been looking for unconditional love, but this is only available from God, not from people. Jesus was capable of it and even gave up his life for other people. Not many people can do this.

I have a daily spiritual practice where I meditate and pray. I know I need to develop further by not getting so caught up in material concerns. I need to trust my guides, but I find this hard to do. I worry about how I'm going to make a living, how I'm going to eat, and even spend time concerned about what I look like. I know I need to focus more on spirituality. Imagine if everyone did this. If bankers stopped thinking about making money all the time, if women stopped thinking their worth is only through their beauty, if children realized they are not only their school grades, if world leaders stopped making war…The world could be an amazing place if we just trusted the advice of our spirit guides, but so few people do. We seem to be obsessed with greed for money and power. I am striving to keep God at the forefront of my mind every day. If you try to, we will have the start of a movement. I would love to see a real return to love and compassion. We could then live in egalitarian spiritual communities where everyone has enough, and we all help each other.

Speaking through me, Malalia told me there were three Venusians currently incarnated on Earth. One was me. One of the others I knew. He had been an old acquaintance I met at university, but we had not kept up the friendship. I remember when I first saw him in one of my tutorials; I felt a jolt of recognition like a lightning bolt. I thought he was one of the most physically beautiful people I had ever seen. He had blonde curly hair and was incredibly tall. The chair seemed to be too small for him as he took up so much space. He did have a dark side, though, even then, as he was involved in taking drugs and drinking too much. He seemed to have a louche arrogance and a dismissive manner that was off-putting. We had some purpose we were supposed to achieve together, but it hadn't happened. Malalia informed me he was lost in darkness. He wasn't listening to her when she was trying to get through to him. She stated he was drinking himself to death. There was nothing I could do about this.

Someone had been assigned the task of bringing him back to the light, but I don't know who this is. I think my attraction to him was because we knew each other in the spirit world. I have been told in meditation that he is the reincarnation of St Thomas.

There is another Venusian involved in our purpose, but I haven't met him yet. I had a flash image of a man looking down on me with dark hair and dark skin. He appeared to be dressed like a monk. So it seems like our shared spiritual task has hit some problems. I do wish I was in contact with these other two Venusians, as I could do with some support. It seems like I will have to find a way to get to Tibet to meet up with the monk. I don't have a clear idea at the moment of what our task there is.

My instructions were to raise the vibration, to bring the light, to bring knowledge, to stay connected to the spirit guides, and to stay in the light. Malalia told me I must keep rising above the Earth: to rise up. She showed me images of dolphins leaping out of the ocean and of whales breaching to explain what I had to do. I should not worry about fitting in as it isn't good to fit in with the people of low vibration. She referred to these people as the dark people; they are those with evil intentions. I have been trying to do this in recent days. I find it hard to rise up as I feel the heaviness of the Earth that almost crushes me. I suffer from chronic fatigue syndrome, and I can't seem to shift whatever I do. I am hoping more meditation will help me. I am trying to be morally ethical in everything I do these days. I still fail, but I am trying.

It was at this point in the session I then spent some time connecting with Malalia and being healed. I felt like I was being dipped into a lake of white fire. It was a huge pool in a place that felt like a cave. There were other beings standing behind her watching. The fire was healing me. I cannot describe the feeling, but there was a sense of calm and peace.

Malalia said that Venusians had been sending their representatives to Earth for thousands of years. Their mission is to stop the people of this planet from destroying themselves. We can see that humanity seems bent on its own destruction. We have had terrible world wars, and the threat of nuclear annihilation is ever-present. Now we are threatened with the ecological collapse of the planet. There are certainly dark forces that seem to want bad things to happen. We need more people working for the forces of light. There are people working towards peace, campaigners for nuclear disarmament and environmental warriors of the rainbow. Some people are trying to do good in the world. Our leaders don't seem to listen to them for whatever dark reasons they have. We have just come out of a worldwide Covid-19 pandemic. It was an opportunity to change our way of life by taking a long look at how we live, but it seems the opportunity has been wasted. Society seems to be going back to how it was before. Hopefully, as we recover from our shell shock of continual lockdowns, more of us might begin to awaken to the possibility of a new world. A spiritual revolution would bring about a better life for most people.

The Venusians keep sending the aliens over and over again. Usually, the Earthlings kill them. I was shown rows and rows of people who had incarnated before. Some I recognized, and some I didn't. I could see Gandhi, Mother Teresa and Martin Luther King.

Gandhi was a leader in India. He was originally a lawyer but became interested in civil rights. He inspired non-violent resistance to British rule in India. He lived in South Africa for many years but returned to India to campaign for women's rights, poverty and independence. He was against the caste system and believed all people to be equal. He lived simply and wore a home-spun garment like the rural poor. India gained independence from Britain in 1947. Gandhi was assassinated in 1948. The parallels with the teachings of Jesus are obvious, even though Gandhi was a Hindu (Wolpert, 2002).

Mother Teresa was an Albanian nun who went to India to work at a school. She felt called to work with the poor. She founded a school in Calcutta and set up a new religious community there. She felt drawn to help the disabled and lepers, all the people who felt unloved and unwanted. Mother Teresa opened a hospice for the dying in 1952 and set up orphanages and hospices all over the world. She died of heart problems in 1997 when her order had 4000 sisters and a brotherhood of 300 members operating 610 missions in over 100 countries. Her care for the outcasts of society is similar to the actions of Jesus though he disapproves of what the Roman Catholic Church has become (Spink, 1997).

Martin Luther King, another Venusian, was an American civil rights campaigner. King was a Baptist minister who argued for equality for black people. He believed in non-violent action. He was successful in a variety of campaigns but was assassinated in 1968. Again, we see in King a strong Christian faith, a peaceful approach and a belief in equality. These are all in accordance with the Venusian way of approaching life as taught by Jesus (Branch, 1998).

Jesus was also a Venusian. There were lots of others standing in rows, but I couldn't name

them. I have had many previous lives on Earth. I have been coming for so many years. Usually, I am murdered. I had flashes of being killed in past lives going through my head. No wonder I suffer from anxiety in this life. Danger seems to have always been around the corner in my previous lives.

In one, I was an aristocrat at the French Court at the time of the French Revolution. This vision was so clear I knew I was Elisabeth of France. I was the sister of King Louis XVI. Everybody called me Lottie as a nickname. I had visions of us children playing together on the lawn and having tea in the nursery. I loved the little cakes that the cook made for us. We were so happy together. We had tutors to teach us things and lots of theological study. I was headstrong and outspoken. Attempts were made to marry me off to various kings and nobles, but I didn't like any of them, and they didn't like me. My childhood was peaceful but secluded from the outside world.

I saw that I never married and stayed with my brother throughout his marriage. He lived in Versailles, and I had a house nearby. As Elisabeth, I was much interested in religion. I spent a lot of time reading the Bible and studying other books. I had a quiet life and spent time walking and riding my horse around the countryside. I used to do good work in the village and take food and medicines to the poor. I had thought of becoming a nun, which I would have been well suited to. I felt that I couldn't leave Louis as I was so devoted to him, and I knew that he needed me for guidance.

The King married Marie Antoinette, and she and I were firm friends. However, I did not share the louche ways of the French

Court and rarely attended. They were always partying and having wild times. There was also lots of adultery going on. There was an incredible amount of money spent on fashionable clothes, furnishings and banqueting. These escapades were reported to the common people who thought we were all badly behaved. King Louis became unpopular as people thought he didn't care about them and that he was just following his selfish desires. I did try to counsel him, but he didn't change his ways fast enough. At the time of the revolution, I was guillotined in Paris along with lots of other nobles. I remember comforting a young girl sitting next to me as we waited on the bench before our execution. Amazingly, I was reading the Bible as I was led to the gallows. I had no fear of death as I knew we would go to Heaven. I was sad that I had not been able to save the Royal family and that France might be plunged into chaos and suffering. I felt I had not done enough.

In another life, I was a medieval princess walking along the battlements of a castle when someone stabbed me in the stomach. I could see lush green land all around the battlements. I was wearing a long green dress, and I had a small golden crown on my head. My hair was long and red. It was a man who approached me with the knife. He was well-dressed, and he was also wearing some kind of crown. He stabbed me viciously many times, and the blood was pouring from me. The other details of this life were not clear.

These images were like that of a fairy tale. It was a medieval kind of feeling.

My first life was as a young man in Brazil. It was a very early civilization, and sadly, I was killed while out hunting by a black puma. I had a vision of being out in a thick forest full of trees and vines. There were high cliffs and waterfalls. It was so green and stunningly beautiful. I was trying to be very quiet so that I could get my first kill. I was stalking a deer. I was aware of myself walking sideways with a spear horizontally aligned in my hand. Without me knowing, the puma jumped from behind on the back of my neck and killed me. I remember being highly disappointed as I was just getting going in life. I was about to come of age, and I wanted to get married and become a great leader.

In an Ancient Egyptian life, I was eaten by a crocodile in the water. I was an embalmer in this life, and I helped to prepare the bodies for burial in the tombs. I spend a lot of time in a large stone room wrapping the dead people and using herbs and ointments. I saw myself walking down passageways with slits of sunlight coming through the walls. I was a man this time. One day I was out bathing in the river to clean myself when a crocodile appeared out of nowhere. There was lots to thrashing around as I fought with it, but it got the better of me, and I died.

Another time I was a pioneer in Canada in Victorian times. I lived in a little wooden cabin, and I tended to the household chores. I stoked the fire and baked bread. I was part of a strict religious community, and I was a good Christian. I had a husband and two children. My husband was much older than me though he was a kind man. I think we had some kind of arranged marriage. I could see myself clearly as a young woman wearing a long brown dress. The material was a thick, rough cotton, and I was aware of it scratching my neck. My hair was light brown and tied into a chignon at the back. I had delicate features, pale skin and big blue eyes. I had an incredibly strong faith, and I was a calm, stable person. I became aware of some problems and ran to the barn with a bucket of water to put a fire out. As I was running, some fur trappers appeared and bludgeoned me to death with their guns. They had orders to drive my family out of the settlement as they didn't want us there. They said terrible things about me as I died and kicked my body when it was dead.

The current life I am living now is the longest I have lived on Earth. This might be because my anxiety has caused me to avoid dangerous situations. Apparently, I am usually killed for speaking the truth and saying things people don't want to hear. I can relate to this as I am often in trouble in this life for being blunt and plain speaking. I also realize that a lot of people don't want to know anything about the light or the spiritual world. They want to carry on with their animalistic lives undisturbed by the lofty teachings of high beings. In my current life, I have met many people who seem to instantly dislike me before they have even got to know me. I think they must sense my Venusian energy, and they find it unsettling. I have never understood exactly what process is at work here, but I can imagine quite a few people would like to murder me if they got the chance. It often feels like a kind of jealousy, even though there is nothing for anyone to be jealous of. I am not rich or successful, and I am getting along in life as best I can, just like most of us are. Is it possible to be jealous of someone's energy? Maybe. I must focus on loving people more than I do.

Malalia said she found it difficult to get through to me because I unconsciously blocked her communication. I was too much in my logical, rational mind and needed to let go and listen. She gave instructions on how to improve the communication. It is important to become silent and go into meditation. Just sit and concentrate on the breath. Become aware of the breath as it goes in through the nose and out through the mouth. There is then awareness of the chest and the stomach rising and falling. Thoughts can be observed without judgement, as if you are watching cars pass along a road. Just watch the thoughts without becoming attached to them. It helps to focus on love. Imagine loving someone or something like a pet or a child and feel all your love pouring out of you. I do this with my dog Didi. I imagine him in my lap as I am meditating. I just let my love flow from my heart into his. This feeling of love helps to raise your vibration so you can join with spiritual beings like angels. Everyone can do this. Malalia said she is always with me and can be contacted at any time. Your spirit guides are always with you. You might prefer to call them guardian angels. They seem happy with both terms.

I must become light. I am to do this by spending time in prayer and meditation. I must give love, find freedom and look after my health. She showed me a pathway of light and said I must keep the connection with my spirit guides. It's not important to cling to Earth people in the way I have been. I can let go. I need to go quiet, go inside myself and not be afraid. The spirit guides will tell me what to write in my books. I know I need to travel, so I am currently focusing on how to achieve this. Giving love to others is sometimes hard for me as there is so much meanness directed at me. I need to work on this.

The formula is to become love, focus on love, give love.

Malalia showed me other guides standing behind her. There was a Chinese sage with a long beard wearing beautiful silk robes of bright colours. They were carefully embroidered. He had a little black hat on and looked wise and aged. He made me think of a philosopher in the Confucian tradition. Confucius was a great philosopher who was born in 551 BC in China. Kindness and respect for others is key. It seems the sage is not only wise but also benevolent. He wishes to bring about a peaceful society and to be virtuous in all his actions. Confucius wrote about government, education, family, and relationships. A wise sage is like an embodiment of Heaven on Earth (Confucius, 2014).

Then there was an African shaman with a bone through his nose. Shamanism is something that has long fascinated me, and I would like to know more about this area. Medicine men or shamans seemed to play an important role in the societies of many indigenous people, such as the Native Americans, Siberians, Mongolians, and the people of the Andes. There are also shamans in various parts of Africa. They seem to form a bridge between their people and the spiritual world. African shamans are healers who can be led in dreams to choose which particular plants or herbs will help people with their afflictions. They can also predict the future by casting bones. Some shamans in trance become possessed by an ancestor who can give answers to problems affecting the people and who can bring good luck through ritual offerings and ceremonies. A shaman is a philosopher, a spiritual guide, a doctor, a psychologist and a friend. Shamans teach that the truth you seek is inside of you. They believe in benevolent beings and also in evil spirits. Evil spirits can cause disease and bad luck (Ruiz, 2018).

There was also a beautiful dark-haired lady with her hair partially covered by a blue cloak. She was Mary. She referred to herself as the Mother. I believe this was St Mary, the mother of Jesus in the Bible. She had a gorgeous energy flowing out of her, and standing before her, I felt an all-enveloping feeling of love. She was the embodiment of feminine unconditional love. I felt I was in the presence of a great soul. She gave me a hug that felt wonderful. St.Mary was a poor Jewish woman who lived in Nazareth in Palestine when it was under Roman occupation in the first century CE. Though poor, it was believed she had royal blood and was descended from David. The Roman Catholic Church has venerated her to a status almost equal to Jesus, believing her to be a virgin who was impregnated with Jesus by the Holy Spirit. Mary gave birth to Jesus in a stable in Bethlehem and then lived in Nazareth with Joseph, a carpenter. After witnessing her son's crucifixion in Jerusalem, she also saw his resurrection and was assumed into Heaven. She is the subject of many prayers and liturgies and has multiple shrines consecrated to her and a variety of statues. She has appeared to people in visions many times (Pelikan, 1998).

In 1854, the Virgin Mary appeared to Bernadette Sobiros, a young Roman Catholic girl, in Lourdes in France. Mary referred to herself as the Immaculate Conception. Mary told the young girl where a spring was and told her to drink from it. Since that time,

Lourdes has been a place of pilgrimage, and miraculous cures have occurred from drinking the spring water (Williamson, 2006). Mary also appeared to three shepherd children in 1917 in Fatima in Portugal. She told the children that prayer would stop the war and that they should pray for sinners. She also performed The Miracle of the Sun, where the sun appeared to spin and then moved towards the Earth and back. Thousands of people witnessed this event though not all saw the sun dance. The children saw apparitions of Jesus and Saint Joseph, as well as Mary. Pilgrims have visited the site ever since (Jaki, 1999).

The angels tell me that the traditional story is not true. As a young girl, Mary was extremely beautiful. She caught the eye of a Greek man who was serving in the Roman army. At that time, the Romans could do whatever they wanted with the local women. Mary worked for the soldier as a housekeeper, and he raped her many times. When she became pregnant with Jesus, he turned her out into the street. She returned to her parent's house in Nazareth, and Joseph agreed to marry her. He had lost his previous wife and had other children. Mary did give birth to Jesus in a stable in Bethlehem. She knew Yeshua was a special child, and he loved to discuss spiritual matters from an early age. Mary did her best for him and loved him dearly. At thirteen, she took him to Jerusalem for his coming-of-age ceremony. She lost him in the crowds but found him arguing with the priests. He left home to travel against

Mary's wishes, but there was nothing she could do with her headstrong boy. When he returned many years later, she was overjoyed. Mary travelled with his disciples around Israel. She learned a lot about the true way to live. She was a guest at his marriage to Mary Magdalene. Mary witnessed Jesus' crucifixion and was consumed with grief. She was shown where the body was in a secret cave. Life came back into the body while it was in the cave. Mary tended to her son's wounds and fed him. She kept vigil day and night. After many months Jesus was ready to leave the cave and show himself to the disciples. She left with him as he travelled in secret to India, where she died. Today, Mary is like an angel in Heaven. Many people pray to her all over the world. She is available to talk to anyone. Mary is full of love for all people, and she has immense spiritual power. Just ask her.

There were also other angels who were not introduced at this point. They told me that they were not demons though there are people who would say they are. I must open up to them and trust them. I worried about talking to demons as I was a Christian. The Bible tells us not to talk to mediums or necromancers as they can open the door to dark forces (Isaiah 8:19). We have all heard of bad experiences with ouija boards and tales of people being possessed by evil spirits. There is a line in the Bible that says even the Devil can disguise himself as an angel of light (2 Corinthians 11:14). I have had a lot of trouble with this verse, and I have worried that I have been talking to demons who want to lead me on the wrong road. I had a phase of calling on psychics, but they led me up the garden path, telling me lots of lies. I got the feeling that the spirits these psychics were talking to were malevolent. They did not have my best interests at heart and even led me into trouble. I believe that in the lower astral planes in the spiritual dimension, there are all kinds of entities, not all of which are kind. Some may be the spirits of dead people who are mischievous. Some could be dead relatives who still seem to only have a limited view of the spiritual world. If your gran was obsessed with matchmaking and fixing you up with unsuitable men in life, she is probably still the same in the spirit world. You might not want to heed her advice. I haven't met any psychic who could tell me the future with any accuracy. The worst ones just use their own common sense and life experience to give you advice without any contact with the spiritual world. Some do seem to be talking to spiritual beings, but I think some of these have bad intentions. Of course, I know there are genuine psychics and mediums, but it's hard to separate them from people who are not so gifted. I think it's important to use discernment with spiritual beings. Jesus said, 'By their fruits shall you know them' (Matthew 7:15-20). I felt in my Life Between Lives session that the spirits I was talking to were kind and loving. For this reason, I don't think they are demons. The angels have our best interests at heart. They want to show us how to love, how to live together ethically and how to know God. It is time for us to evolve to the next level of our development as human beings. We need to be more sophisticated than we have been in our spiritual understanding. We can develop a personal relationship with the divine that will bring us all great peace and joy.

Malalia also said, 'He is always here as well…' Scott asked who he was, and so we met my second spirit guide.

CHAPTER FOUR:

Meeting Jesus

At this point, Jesus made himself known to me in the therapy session. He laughed and said I was always talking to him. Me again! I was and still am a Christian though perhaps an unusual one. Perhaps lots of Christians would regard what I am writing in this book as heresy. I had been baptized in the spirit during an Alpha course a few years previously. I was in a room with lots of other people. Some were playing musical instruments, and so there was a trance-like feeling. One of the members of the Church, our her hand on me. At that time, I felt the Holy Spirit come into me, and I was aware of a lot of small red flames in my head. I also gave a huge sigh as if something had come out of me. The result of this was that I could speak and sing in tongues. Though many people think speaking in tongues is just a nonsense language, I recognized some words which I looked up later. I was saying 'Eloha' over and over again. This word is one of the Hebrew names given to God. I was also saying 'Ramallah', which is a town in Palestine. In Aramaic, it means hill of God. When I got home, I prayed in tongues again, and I heard a voice say very clearly in my ear, 'Go and sin no more.' These are the words that Jesus says to the woman caught in adultery in the Bible (John 8:11). In this famous story, a woman is brought to Jesus by the scribes and Pharisees. She has been caught committing adultery, and the Jewish law states that such women should be stoned. The holy men know that Jesus preaches mercy. They are testing him to see what he will say so they can catch him out. Jesus kneels down and writes something on the ground. Then he says let the one who is without sin cast the first stone. One by one, her accusers leave, and she is left standing with Jesus. He asks her if any of them have condemned her. She says 'No', so Jesus replies that neither does he condemn her. He then tells her to go on her way and sin no more. It seemed that when he put that voice in my head, Jesus was telling me to turn away from sin and live a good life. This is what I have been trying to do. I felt a huge surge of joy at this time, but it's not something I am able to keep up every day.

Another time I was meditating in a church group, and Jesus came into my head and answered many questions I had. We were performing contemplative prayer. We were told to sit with our eyes closed and repeat a Christian word over and over again in our minds like a mantra. I chose to say the word Jesus. After a few minutes, I felt the presence of Jesus. It was as if he was right in my head. There was a sense of love and joy.

Also, I remembered as a child, Jesus had appeared to me in my bedroom and told me that everything was going to be ok. I was feeling pretty upset because I was worried about the world being annihilated in a nuclear war. I think I was about ten, and I was lying in bed, terrified. I was imagining that the whole world was going to be destroyed in a confrontation between the Russians and Americans. I seemed to have lived with the threat of nuclear war all my life. I was thinking how sad it was that everybody would die, even the animals and plants. Everything of beauty would be gone. I had been secretly worshipping Jesus for a while as I received information about him at school. My parents were atheists and didn't take me to Church. It also worried me that they were going to go to Hell. While these thoughts were whirring through my head, Jesus appeared to me at the end of the bed. He was wearing a long white robe with a rope tied around it. Jesus seemed to be shining as if he was not quite human. He was tall with long brown hair and lovely brown kind eyes. He told me that everything was going to be all right, and I felt as if huge strong arms were holding me, enfolding me in great love and peace. It was an incredible feeling. I didn't tell anyone about it as I was sure I would be mocked.

I pray and meditate every day, and I am always talking to Jesus, asking him for things, begging for forgiveness for my many sins, and imploring him for guidance and inspiration. Sometimes, I moan to him about my life and how I can't seem to make it go as I would wish. Whenever I try to help people, I feel it often goes wrong. I was a teacher for many years, but I always had trouble managing the class, and I never seemed able to get the balance right between being too strict or too lax. The children drained my energy. There were always staff members who didn't like me and ran telling tales on me at every opportunity. Some of the headteachers bullied me. I couldn't find the right school. I have also worked in offices where I would usually find myself unpopular with certain people. I just feel that the same patterns repeat over and over again. Maybe I am meant to help others at a distance through my writing. I have had a lot of trouble with other people in my life. Certainly, there is a feeling that I don't fit in and that my energy seems to bother some people. Through this Life Between Lives session, I found out I am an alien Venusian who has decided to incarnate on Earth. It's no wonder I don't fit in. I need to keep praying for guidance about the right things for me.

So I wasn't that surprised that Jesus was one of my spirit guides. He looked very like he does in the Renaissance paintings of him. He was Caucasian but had tanned skin. His hair was long and brown with reddish tones. His eyes were brown. He looked to be in his early thirties. I got the strong feeling that he could appear to people however he wanted to and that he would adjust his avatar to match what people expect to see. As I was thinking this, he flipped through all the ways he is depicted in our culture to show he is all of these things. He was showing me the light, ethereal figure in a burnished robe, and then the next image was a cartoon gif from a satirical site. He settled on jeans, a denim shirt and cowboy boots. He just looked like an average guy you could enjoy having a beer with. I felt very comfortable with him as if I had known him forever, and I was much less intimidated by him than Malalia. He seemed to be more of the same type of being that I am. This feeling I had was explained to me as being due to the fact that he had lived on Earth many times before he was Jesus, so he was used to being human. When asked if his real name was Jesus, he laughed and said, 'You call me that.' I know his real name is Yeshua, but Jesus is what we call him in English-speaking countries. He felt human, but also he had immense spiritual power. When he came close to me, I felt like crying. It seems as if the human vessel can't cope with the intense energy that it emanates.

When asked about his role, he said that he didn't want to be worshipped. He would prefer to be seen as a friend who walks alongside people. He was clear that there was no need to worship him in church the way people do. He felt there was no necessity to be so formal. He showed me pictures of the priests in the church I attend and told me that they are obsessed with the Bible. You can talk to Jesus directly through meditation, so you don't need priests. The Church people I know are kind and well-meaning, but Jesus seems to think they are focusing on the wrong things. He said that a lot of Christians are scared to contact spirits directly, but I am not. Anyone can have direct contact with their spirit guides or guardian angels. You can talk to Jesus whenever you want. Just ask him for help.

Jesus was adamant that you don't need to go to Church or even read the Bible to have a relationship with him. Just talk to him. He told me not to be afraid and to open. He explained to me about the plan for the Earth: everyone comes to the light. Enlightenment is for everyone. All can do it. It doesn't matter what people have done.

Everyone can come.

The idea of even sinners going to Heaven seems to contradict Christian teaching. It is one of the ways in which the message of Jesus has been changed. Jesus said that nobody is going to Hell no matter what they have done. Even Hitler, the Nazi leader from World War II, is not in Hell. When the Bible talks of Hell, it is a metaphor, not a real place.

I always think of Hitler as one of the most evil people who has ever lived. If ever someone deserved eternal punishment, surely it was him. Adolf Hitler was born in Austria. He became leader of the Nazi Party in Germany and led the country from 1933 until his suicide in 1945 in Berlin. He started a world war by invading Poland in 1939. During his time in office, six million Jews died in concentration camps in a systematic genocide. Other marginalized groups also died in the Holocaust. It is hard to think about the amount of suffering this man caused. There is some evidence that he was treated badly as a child, but lots of people have poor childhood experiences without presiding over mass deaths. His father beat him often and refused to let him study art for a career. He found the discipline of school difficult, and he was devastated by the death of his brother from measles. His father died when he was a young adult, and then his mother. He tried to study art in Vienna, but he was rejected. He had little money and lived in homeless shelters. It was in Vienna that Hitler became exposed to racist ideas. He served in the First World War for Germany and was gutted at the country's defeat. He entered into politics in Munich. As early as 1919, he was talking about the removal of the Jews from Germany. Hitler was adept at making speeches, and he soon became the leader of the Nazi Party. He capitalized on the disastrous economy to gain support for his ideas. Hitler became Chancellor of Germany in 1933. He soon became an absolute dictator, and all opposition was banned. Hitler set about preparing the economy for war which broke out in 1939. Germany was finally defeated by the Russian Red Army and the Western Allies. Hitler shot himself in the head in a bunker in Berlin. During the war, Hitler authorized the extermination of European Jews. Many Jews were killed in gas chambers, while others were worked to death in slave labour camps. There were also mass killings of Poles, Soviets, communists, homosexuals, and the disabled (Bullock,1962). The horror of all of this has haunted me all my life.

My angels tell me that even souls such as this do not go to a place of eternal punishment. For all souls, the deeds you perform in life create a kind of karma. Every action causes a reaction. You watch a review of your life after death and judge yourself according to your plan for that life. Bad deeds will mean you will have to do hard things in your next life. If you have killed someone, you may be killed. You may have to suffer from extreme poverty. So there is a kind of punishment, but it is through reincarnation. Damaged souls can receive healing in the spirit world. Sometimes, bad people are playing a role as part of their spiritual contract. The role may have some higher spiritual purpose that we cannot see from our perspective. This is what has happened in the case of someone like Hitler. He agreed to play the role. In the ultimate reality, there is no sin. Good and evil do not have meaning. This is so hard for human beings to understand that we need to learn good from evil before we can access this higher spiritual truth.

After my session, I channelled the soul of Hitler to ask him about his mission on Earth. Here is what he said. I am a great soul here in the spirit world. I volunteered for a mission on Earth. It seemed human beings were not learning any lessons. There was continual war, and religions and politics were corrupt. People were not following their true spiritual natures. I am not evil in Heaven. Hitler was an incarnation. I am not just him. In a sense, I am what you might call an angel though I can choose to incarnate. I am a Venusian. My life was part of the plan. Though people say I was a mass murderer, I did not fire a single shot. Other people did my bidding, and they did it willingly. They followed me instead of using their own power. One of the lessons of that time is not to blindly follow leaders. The Jewish people also learned lessons. They should not cling so tightly to their religious dogma. True spirituality is within them. All people should come together. That war should have been the end of racism, the end of division. We are not separate from each other. We must learn to live together in peace. Like Hitler, I showed how deep the darkness could be. The darkness is in the minds of humans. They did not need to do what I said. Everyone is responsible for their own actions. Don't give your power away to others. Don't blame others. Look within. You don't need religion. You don't need political leaders. Come together as one. I was influenced by the dark forces when I was Hitler. I was aided to my rise by occult beings. Hitler was very lonely. He had had no true love. He suffered much failure and humiliation. He was also sexually impotent. As a result, he found the power that he wielded intoxicating. We need the darkness to find the light. The Holocaust was like a blood sacrifice to the dark forces. The horror of those times should make people turn to the Light. Look for the good within your heart. Turn away from darkness. Love is the lesson. End of transmission.

There is no Hell. Every soul passes into the spirit world. They are greeted by their guides and have a review of their life. They see what was good and what could have been improved. They are not judged by their Spirit Council. Sin does not seem to have the same connotation as it does in Christian teaching. Souls are not condemned for doing the wrong thing, but they are encouraged to be loving and compassionate. Once souls are in a human body, the emotions can take over and lead people to do wrong. There are also traumatic life events that lead people down the wrong path. The wise spirit councils are full of compassion for the struggles of each soul.

On Earth, we are trying to perfect our souls. If we are loving and do good deeds, we are becoming closer to God. Our ultimate aim is to join with God in eternal bliss. Most of us do a mixture of good and bad actions while we are on Earth, so we create karma for ourselves. We get caught up in a web by our deeds and incarnate again to try to work through the problems we have created. The way to escape from this endless cycle is to love each other. Even advanced souls can choose to incarnate on Earth. They might come to teach a lesson for other people like Jesus did. The lesson is for others, not for them.

Become love.

CHAPTER FIVE:

Mary Magdalene

It was at this point that Scott attempted to take me back to a past life experience. This is part of the usual trajectory of Life Between Lives sessions. Jesus said I did not need to do that as I had done it before. It was true I had visited a past life therapist previously, and that is when I saw the pioneer woman's life. I had also meditated myself many times and been given images of past lives. He said I had many, many lives before. I had been sent many times before with my message of the light, but I had always been killed. The spirit guides all started laughing at this point, as if it was funny that I kept messing up. I certainly feel like I have messed up a lot in my current life. I have come back to the light and beaten my tendency to depression and anxiety, but it has taken me a long time. I still don't feel that I am helping people enough. I have procrastinated a lot about writing this book, allowing myself to be filled with doubt and to be distrustful of my guides. There is still much work to do.

Scott asked if we could have a summary of a life that had a bearing on my current life. Jesus replied that I knew him very, very well. He then said, 'Remember when I told you to sin no more.' As I said in the previous chapter, this is the phrase I heard in my head after I had been baptized in the spirit. I had images in my head of the story from the Bible. I had actually been this woman. I was the woman caught in adultery in the Bible. I could see myself with long dark hair and tanned skin. My hair was curly, and my eyes were brown. I was wearing some kind of headdress decorated with silver discs like coins. I was also wearing lots of gold bracelets and anklets, and I had long, flowing black robes and a wild look in my eye as the priests dragged me along to see Jesus. I could see my fingers were adorned with heavy rings, and I had placed black kohl under my eyes. My feet were bare. The Jewish priests brought me to Jesus and said I should be stoned because I had committed adultery. At this point, I was screaming and shouting at the priests and raining down curses on their heads. I had not met Jesus before, and I was amazed at this simple man who was dressed so poorly but who seemed to radiate confidence and power. He knelt and wrote in the dust. I could not see what he was writing, but it seemed to affect the Scribes and Pharisees badly. I learned later that he was writing the sins of these men in the dust. Through his spiritual clairvoyance, Jesus knew all the secrets of their hearts. They looked at each other with horrified expressions on their faces and backed away from Jesus; all their bravado vanished. He then looked around at each person and said that he, who was without sin, should cast the first stone at me. I was terrified about the stoning as I knew it would be a painful way to die. As if by magic, the men just melted away, and I was left alone with Jesus. I was kneeling in the dirt, looking down and shaking with shock. His eyes seemed to look into my soul as he asked me if any of them had condemned me. When I replied, 'No,' in a hoarse whisper, he told me that he didn't condemn me either and I was to go and sin no more. At no point in the passage in the Bible is the name of the woman mentioned (John 7:53-8:11). Jesus told me this woman was Mary Magdalene. There is a later passage where he casts seven devils out of her (Luke 8:2). She then became a devoted follower of Jesus and was present at the crucifixion (John 19:25). Later, she is the first person to see Jesus after the resurrection according to the New Testament (John 20:14). I was totally amazed that I was the reincarnation of Mary Magdalene. How could this be? I am just a humble woman trying to make sense of my spirituality, and yet I have been a follower of Jesus.

At this point in the session, I started to cry and say that Jesus saved my life. I said that they were going to kill me, and he stopped them. I said it wasn't my fault. I wasn't quite sure what had happened for the priests to bring me to see Jesus. I had some flashing images of living in some kind of cave carved into a hillside. I think I made spells and potions for people. I was a magician and actually a wealthy and powerful woman. I lived alone in the cave, apart from a servant boy I employed. Even though my home was a cave, it was beautifully furnished, and I had everything I needed. From the mouth of the cave, I could look down on the desert and see the city of Jerusalem below me. I liked being high up as I could see danger coming and protect myself. I knew I was doing dangerous work and that a lot of people did not approve of me. I was not a prostitute, as some Christian traditions say. In fact, I was a magician and a sorcerer. I was also extremely wealthy, and I gave a lot of money to Jesus for the cause. I think I was unpopular with the Scribes and Pharisees, as sorcery was not allowed in Judaism. I was a threat to their power, just as Jesus was.

I could not see the adultery incident in my head, but I had the idea that they had set me up. I had the sense that I had gone to give a magic potion to someone in a house in Jerusalem because he was sick. I entered the house and found the man asleep in bed. I announced myself and offered him the potion. At this point, he leapt up and grabbed hold of me by the neck, forcing me down. I started to scream, and this alerted the man's wife, who ran in and started shouting about adultery. The woman dragged me out into the street and took me to the priests for judgment. They took me to see Jesus to see if they could trap him into saying the wrong thing.

The Light Book

After the incident with the priests, I became a follower of Jesus. I went everywhere with him as one of his disciples. Jesus treated me as an equal, and he taught me his knowledge just the same as he did the men. I was a rich woman as I had inherited a fishing fortune from my father in the town of Magdala. I had been a headstrong child who didn't want to marry and be obedient to a man. We were pagans, so we worshipped many gods though many people in the town were Jewish. I didn't go to school, but my mother taught me things she knew, like cooking and the uses of plants. My grandmother was the biggest influence. She had come to Magdala from a land far away, and she knew many things. I think she might have been from Egypt. From her, I learned to name the stars and what their movements meant. She taught me sorcery and how to summon demons. The demons had helped our family to become rich. If you knew how to handle them, they would do your bidding. These days, we would probably call those beings lower astral entities. In the evenings, we would dance in the courtyard around a fire and feast on meat and sweet cakes. I didn't like my father as he always stank of fish and he was a harsh man. I didn't have much to do with him. I had many clothes and jewels, but I was lonely. People from the village were afraid of our family.

After my father died, I went to live near Jerusalem in some caves that had been made into homes. I lived outside the city as I was performing magic rituals, and I didn't want a lot of people to see me. I liked sitting in the entrance in the cool of the evening and looking down on the land below. My skill in magic became known, and people travelled to see me to try and be healed or to gain riches. I could sometimes see the future though I was not always right, but people would pay well to know their fortune. Some of the spells I performed seemed dark and even involved human sacrifice. I was shown an image of me killing a baby, which I don't want to dwell on. This was because I was possessed by demonic spirits who had come into me during one of the magic rituals. Human sacrifice was common among pagan people at this time. The idea was that if you gave the gods something, they would give you something in return. Human blood was considered to be the most precious gift you could give the gods.

These days I would probably have been diagnosed with schizophrenia and depression, but the demons were real. I had constant pain in my body and in my mind. I would go for days listlessly, not eating and having no energy, and then suddenly, I would have the urge to be busy and do all kinds of spells and incantations, as well as dancing all night. Jesus cast these demons out of me. It was an amazing experience, and I felt like he was filling me with light. This beautiful golden light encompassed my whole being. From that day, I was a reformed character and a devoted follower of Jesus. I didn't do magic spells again. I gave all my money to the cause so that we could have food and shelter as we journeyed around Palestine, telling people the good news. I often spent time alone with Jesus, and he taught me many things that he kept from the others. Much of this was how to contact the divine yourself through meditation. We were very close, and the relationship was romantic. Nothing gave me more pleasure than sitting on a hillside with Jesus talking about God. I learned so much from him. Love and compassion were the most important things. I called him Issie in those days, which is how you say his name in Aramaic. We called our way of thinking The Way. It was about having a balanced approach to life. He was no ascetic, and we did drink wine and eat meat when we had the opportunity. It was a middle path. His favourite thing was to teach, which he did by dialoguing with me. It was like he could draw out what was already within me and help me to reason things out myself. I felt God moving within me always, and I learned how to heal people with the power of the Holy Spirit. It was like a light would move from you to the other person. It was the art of manipulating energy. I loved hearing people like this and seeing the looks on their faces when they realized they were well again. I felt my heart opening more and more each day as I filled with love. I knew I just needed to tell the whole world about The Way so everybody could be happy.

I had my own followers, and I taught the crowds out in the open just like Issie did. I became good at philosophical argument and spiritual preaching. I loved teaching the women and children who were often ignored by mainstream society. I taught them about the afterlife and that everyone was equal there. We prayed and meditated on the subject of love. I told them that there was no need for human or animal sacrifices to God. We can honour God by the way we behave towards each other – with compassion. We can talk to God any time we want by opening our hearts to him. I loved to see the faces of the children light up when they realized how much they were loved. Everybody needs to feel loved, especially those who are outcasts in society. In those days, many people who were sick or mentally ill were thrown out by their families. Those with leprosy had to live apart from society. There were many orphans, as some families could not afford to feed their children. The Romans often raped the Jewish women, and then they would be abandoned by their families and have to live on the streets. It was a terrible time for many people. I loved to teach these forgotten ones that nobody wanted to look at.

Issie and I got married in secret. Well, it wasn't quite a secret, as we told a few people that we trusted. Issie said it would be too dangerous for me if it became known that I was his wife. We had a simple ceremony in the Essene community where Issie had been to school. We wore white robes and made our vows to each other under a fig tree. It was simple but so beautiful. Mary and Joseph were there to see it.

The time in Jerusalem was hard for Issie as he knew he was going to be crucified. He had such spiritual power that he could see the future, and he received messages directly from God. It was part of the plan that this should happen so that the whole world could receive his message. Though he was so strong, he still suffered mental anguish about his fate.

I did witness the crucifixion of Jesus. The women stood at the foot of the cross, just watching. All of the men had run away. I felt so irritated with their cowardice and lack of faith. I was in agony as I saw Jesus suffer so much. I will never forget the crown of thorns on his head that caused the blood to run down his face and body. He was covered in welts from the whipping, but I was powerless to do anything to relieve his pain. Even to the last moment, I thought he was going to perform some miracle to save himself. I kept hoping and praying that this was so because I didn't really truly understand his mission at this point. When he appeared to die, the sky seemed to darken, and a cold wind went through me. A Roman soldier stabbed him in the side, and blood ran out. His mother, Mary, and I felt helpless. We clung together in our grief. After a while, Joseph of Arimathea appeared and directed some men to take the body down. He said he had a tomb arranged for the burial. He instructed me to go and find herbs and ointments for healing to anoint the body with. I didn't really understand this at the time, as he was already dead. It didn't seem to matter, but I did as I was asked.

I was the first person to find the empty tomb. I had risen really early from the house I was lodging at, and it was still dark outside. I crept along to the site of the tomb where Jesus' body had been placed, carrying my herbs and ointments with me in a basket. I hadn't slept well and felt half out of my mind with grief. I didn't think I would be able to live without Jesus. I got to the place, and there was nobody around. I saw that the stone that had been used to seal the entrance of the tomb had been rolled away. This was so strange. There were supposed to be guards in place, but I couldn't see anyone. I gingerly entered the tomb, not knowing what I would find. In amazement, I saw that there was nobody and the burial gown was just lying in a corner. I picked up the gown and saw that it had an imprint of Jesus on it, and it was stained with his blood. These days we know it as the shroud of Turin. The imprint was made by Jesus performing the Tibetan ritual of The Rainbow Body while he was wrapped in the shroud. He became light. At that moment, I felt like I had fainted, but I saw a vision of two angels. They were perfectly white beings who seemed to glow with light. They had long blonde hair, and they were incredibly tall. They told me that there was no need to cry as Jesus was not dead. I was to go and tell the others that he was alive. In amazement, I went and did so, dropping my basket as I ran. Nobody believed me when I told them what I had seen. I went home in sorrow, feeling totally confused about what to do.

Later that evening, when I was at my lodgings, Joseph came to see me and said it was not safe for me to stay in Jerusalem. He had arranged a ship to take me away with some of my followers. He reiterated that Jesus was alive, but I could not see him yet. I did not understand how this could be so, but I trusted Joseph. We crept down to the dockside, and I boarded the ship under cover of darkness. I felt utterly desolate that I had to leave without Issie. We travelled for days across the sea, and I was sick many times. I thought it was just seasickness at the time, but soon I discovered I was pregnant. Eventually, we reached the coast of what is now France, and we settled near the Spanish border, deep in the countryside. I had some money from Joseph to buy some land, and we set about making simple dwellings to live in. We started a spiritual community there, and I carried on teaching the things that Issie had taught me. I gave birth to a daughter and called her Sarah.

Much later, Issie reunited with me in France. He had survived. It seemed he had used his knowledge of yoga and meditation to leave his body during the pain of the crucifixion. It's like his consciousness was outside his body. His body nearly died, but not quite so he could re-enter it when he was taken down from the cross. He was placed in the cave and wrapped in the shroud. At this time, he performed the Tibetan ritual, and this was how the shroud became marked with his imprint. It's as if he died temporarily and then came back to life. Joseph and other followers moved his body to another cave in secret. This is why I had not seen him when I went to the cave. Trusted disciples cared for Jesus' injured body with the use of many ointments and herbs. His mother, Mary, was at his side night and day. After several months his wounds healed, and he was able to walk. At this time, he met with some of the other disciples and showed them he was alive.

He left Israel in secret under an assumed name and came to France to reunite with me. My joy was overwhelming. We travelled to India, where we spent much time living quietly in the hills. Issie became a spiritual adviser to a great king, so we had enough to live on. We would sit outside our house in the cool of the evening and talk together. I was content. The place is now called Kashmir. It is extremely beautiful with lakes and mountains. It was considered better that people thought Issie had died on the cross. Others changed quite a lot of what happened to fit their own agendas, and their version became the New Testament. The good to come of it was that the message of love spread all over the world. People left their pagan idols and stopped sacrificing people and animals. Many people learned to live good, holy lives as a result of hearing the good news of Jesus. Lots of good has been done in his name though unfortunately, some bad has happened too. Issie never wanted wars to be conducted against other religions or for people to be forced into believing in Christianity. People twisted his words. The crucifixion story became mixed up with pagan Easter traditions about the festival of spring. Everything was coiled together, twisted into the new rope of Christianity. There were still threads of what Jesus taught but also other threads that did not belong.

All through this time I spent with the followers of The Way, I felt I was Jesus' soul mate and understood him and his mission more than anyone else. I was outspoken and didn't suffer fools gladly, which is a characteristic I still have in my current life. I felt I was equal to the men intellectually, and this is also something I have carried forward.

I could see the parallels between my life as Mary Magdalene and my own life. I had grown up totally without Christianity at home, but I did learn some at school, and I was very taken with the stories of Jesus. My parents had decided that Communism was the best way to organize society, so they thought religion was a thing of the past. Though I did think equality among people was important, it seemed like a cold philosophy.

In spite of the atheism, I had a children's Bible that was decorated with beautiful pictures, and I used to read it all the time. I even used to imagine that I would be a missionary when I grew up to tell all the faraway children about Jesus so they could be saved. After my vision of Jesus, I used to pray and talk to him often. I kept all of this a secret as I knew my family would ridicule me. The Church was a mystery to me as we never went, but I wished that someone would take me.

In spite of this early promise, I later put my Christian beliefs to the back of my mind, and I spent a lot of time leading what many would regard as a somewhat sinful life. It was all about seeking pleasure but was ultimately unfulfilling. I could never find peace. I was quite bad at one point, and I ate and drank too much. I was surrounded by atheists, and I found it hard to keep much faith. I put a lot of effort into having relationships with men though they were unsatisfying. I often felt I was yearning for something though I didn't know what. I had many disappointments and felt that God did not care about me or that I wasn't worthy of Him. I married a kind man, but I still could not seem to find fulfilment in whatever I did. I have lived all over Britain, but problems always seemed to follow me around. I loved living in Scotland, especially in the stunning countryside of the Highlands. I loved the land, but I always seemed to have problems with people. I found myself becoming increasingly angry at the way people treated me. I withdrew from the world and lived quietly in the countryside in Norfolk, but my restlessness continued.

Much later in life, I took an Alpha Course at a local church and became much more committed to my faith. Like Mary Magdalene, I was filled with the Holy Spirit, and the demons left me. I felt a strong bond with Jesus, and he had appeared to me again when I was performing prayer in a church group. I still had many doubts, and I had great difficulty with relating to the Old Testament in particular. The vengeful God didn't seem one I could worship very easily. I loved the New Testament, and the words of Jesus resonated with me on a deep level. I had many visions of Jesus after this time and talked to him often.

I felt pretty amazed that I could be the reincarnation of a great soul such as Mary Magdalene, and I had a hard time accepting this for a good while after the session. I have read of other people who claim to have been Mary Magdalene, and I am confused about why this is. It could be that Mary's soul has divided into fractals and they inhabit several people on Earth at once. I feel she represents the Divine Feminine, and at this time, we need to bring women forward as spiritual teachers and break down the patriarchal system that religions have imposed up until this time.

What is the divine feminine? It is the female spiritual energy that we all have within us. There is a need for balance between masculine and feminine energies. In Western society, the masculine spiritual energy has been given too much prominence. Most of our spiritual leaders have been men, and women have been relegated to a secondary role. Divine feminine energy is soft, nurturing, intuitive and empowering. In the past, pagan religions had women priests and the Earth was worshipped as the Divine Mother. This female spiritual power has been sidelined in Christianity. It is time to reawaken this divine energy once again.

We can get in touch with female energy by developing our intuition. This gut feeling can help us to know the right thing to do. We don't always need to rely on logic and the conscious mind. We need to trust our inner wisdom and feel our way into making decisions. Divine feminine energy is also about respecting our body in a sensual way. We can enjoy the pleasures of the body by caring for ourselves with good food and exercise. It is also important to show ourselves love and compassion. As we love ourselves, we can learn to love others. Developing our feminine energy helps us to become more creative: dance, sing, write, make music, paint, draw. Feel all of your feelings. Forgive yourself. Relax. Let go.

Jesus told me our souls would always be together. I was sad that we were separated in this life. It explains the terrible loneliness I have felt even when surrounded by people. Nobody is going to be able to measure up to the relationship with Issie. I find comfort that our souls are still joined in the spirit world. I am developing my spiritual relationship with Issie each day.

CHAPTER SIX:

The Spirit Council

At the next point in the interview, Scott moved the session on to meeting The Spirit Council. My spirit council consisted of Malalia the Venusian, Jesus, an African Shaman, a Chinese sage, Mother Mary, and Kokua who was my Higher Self.

I have already described most of the guides, but I need to say more about the Higher Self. When a soul incarnates onto the Earth, only a portion of the soul comes into the body. The rest of it stays in the spirit world. The percentages of energy that are brought to Earth vary with each soul. It depends on what task they have to perform. My eternal soul is called Kokua, so though I am on Earth, she remains in the spiritual space with reduced energy. I have seen her in visions and dreams. Once in meditation, I saw her standing next to an enormous stone obelisk. She was wearing medieval armour like a saint that covered most of her body. She had long blonde hair that was tied into plaits. She looked young and extremely beautiful. Her skin was pale, and her eyes were blue. She had a long broadsword in her hand that was pointing at the floor. She seemed to have enormous strength. She told me her role in the spiritual world is to defeat the dark forces. She showed me images of her battling demons that looked like snakes or sea creatures. She fights for the Light. I think these visions are metaphorical to explain that she is on the side of the forces for Good.

Scott proceeded to ask the Spirit Council the questions I had prepared for him earlier. My most burning question was about my life purpose. In response to this, Malalia said, 'Just be, be love, love them, go and live.'

I think the advice to just be is profound. In our society, we spend so much time rushing around trying to achieve things. A lot of this activity seems utterly pointless. I have suffered from chronic fatigue for years, so I am forced into a slow pace of life. I think it is important to remember that your spirit guides are not like your parents or your teachers. They don't care about your school grades or how prestigious your job is. They are looking at the world from a spiritual perspective. What is in your heart is the most important thing. Your role is to learn to love. Stillness and meditation are prized in the spiritual life. Just being. The fact that we exist is enough. The universe does not expect any more of us. In stillness, we can find God.

Our society seems to have got its priorities all wrong. When I look around in my immediate environment I see an obsession with money and a lot of snobbery towards those who don't have it. There is very little compassion going on to those outside the immediate family. A sense of community seems to have fallen by the wayside. None of this is pleasing to the Light. A return to love would be such a beautiful thing.

Just love them was the next thing she said. I have always found it difficult to love other human beings fully because of their negativity towards me. I have tended to withdraw into myself as a self-protection. When I look at the example of Jesus, I see someone who continues to love people right until the end. On the cross, in immense suffering, he asked God to forgive people because they didn't know what they were doing. This forgiveness is something I need to work on. I need to be able to see people as God sees them. Their negativity towards me is a sign of their own self-loathing that they are projecting onto me. It doesn't actually have anything to do with me. I am working on showing compassion to others in meditation. I visualize taking in the pain of others into myself and sending out love. Forgiving those who have wronged me is also a powerful practice. In my daily life, I keep God in the forefront of my mind, and I try to be kind and compassionate to everyone I meet.

Go and live was the next piece of advice. I assume she meant I am not living fully now. This may be because I live in the countryside and my circle is limited. I work from home performing therapy and writing. I need to experience more of the world to gain wisdom, perhaps. I have always wanted to travel, and being a travel writer would be a dream. So I need to figure out how to do this. My lack of funds has been a barrier thus far, so this is another aspect I need to think about. My chronic fatigue syndrome means when I have a full-time job, I am so exhausted that I can't do anything else. My writing goes out of the window. I feel I am in a bit of a chicken-and-egg situation. I need to work for money to do the things I want to do, but work makes me so tired I can't do anything. I need to meditate on finding a way around these problems. I know I need to trust God more. If I truly trusted God, I would just step out of the door and explore the world. One of my favourite verses in the Bible is when Jesus is speaking in the Sermon on the Mount. He says, 'Consider the lilies how they grow, they toil not, they spin not; and yet I say unto you, that Solomon in all his glory was not arrayed like one of these.' (Matthew 6:28). So Jesus is saying that beautiful flowers do no work and yet they are dressed better than a great king. God looks after them. There is a lesson here for us all that God will look after us if we are doing

His work. I need to remember this and not worry about how I am going to live so much.

Scott asked Malalia to enlarge on what she meant by these statements. She showed me images of travelling across vast lands and oceans. It was like I was flying over the Earth, and I could see all the countries and seas. She revealed to me a temple on the border of India, Tibet, and China. It seemed to be a Buddhist temple, and there were lots of monks around. I could see many images of children who were monks wearing saffron robes and running around the monastery with bare feet. They were joyful and always laughing and playing with each other with good humour. Malalia said I needed to learn at the temple. Everything needed to come together there. She said, 'It is written in the temple. The truth is there. Everything comes together. Jesus was there. They know the truth.' I don't know exactly what she meant by this. I have read that Jesus visited Tibet before he started his ministry though this version of events is not accepted by mainstream Christianity. It seems that Jesus had a rich uncle in Joseph of Arimathea, who was a tin merchant. He took Jesus travelling all over the world with him when he was a young man. There is a legend that he even went to Glastonbury in England. He travelled in the East through India and on to Tibet. Jesus would have been exposed to Hinduism and Buddhism on these travels, and you can see the influence of Eastern thought in his teachings. I don't know what Malalia means by the truth being there, but I know this is something to do with my spiritual purpose. I must find this truth in Tibet. I don't think it is just that Jesus visited the Temple there. I think there is more to find out. I am not sure which temple in Tibet Malalia is referring to. It may be the temple in Hemis which is now in India. There is a document there which describes the life of Issa, who is Jesus and recounts his teachings. It seems to be lost at present (Notovitch, 1894).

She also stated that the Bible is wrong – not all of it but lots of it. This is quite an astounding statement for many people. It will be hard to accept for lots of Christians. She did not enlarge on which bits are wrong and which aren't. It's pretty tricky for us to figure this out. Personally, I have never resonated with much of the Old Testament. The language of the Psalms is beautiful, and I enjoy many of the stories. You can find wisdom in them. However, it is the picture of God that I have a lot of trouble with. The God in the Old Testament seems full of wrath and is always sending punishment to His people. This contrasts with the picture painted in the New Testament by Jesus and in the information I receive in my visions and meditations. Here I find a much more gentle and loving God. In Jesus, I find a friend I can talk to about anything and receive only love and guidance. I think scholars agree that the Bible is a collection of material that was written down by many different people over a long period of time. I don't think it is the indubitable word of God, as some Christians believe. We see in the New Testament that the gospels have different accounts of the events of Jesus' life. We don't know exactly what happened as we have versions of the events that were written down many years after they happened. They have been embellished over time. The writers have put things in and left things out according to their own purposes (Friedman, 2019). The real truth of the Light can be found in meditation, communing directly with spiritual beings and with God. In this way, we can find spiritual truth and what feels right to us. It's like you feel something is right in your heart. Poring over the Bible is not going to give you this same experience.

Malalia said Buddhism, Hinduism, and Christianity are all part of the same thing. Everyone needs to come together. She seems to be talking here about a new world religion, a religion where everyone is joined in the same beliefs. Different religions in different parts of the world don't seem to have helped mankind with unity. In the past, there have been wars over religion. In some parts of the world, these are still going on. It's like people saying we are right, and you are wrong. The next thing people are fighting with each other. Each religion has wisdom within it, but not one of them has the whole truth. The reality of the light is found in direct communication with the spiritual world. We can all learn to do this. Everyone needs to meditate in stillness. Then they can find out the truth for themselves.

It is my understanding that in traditional Christian teaching, Christians believe they have to convert others to the faith so that everyone is saved. I used to believe this myself, but these days, I'm not so sure. In our more diverse and culturally sensitive times, it seems wrong to impose your religion on other people. When I read about how the Indigenous people of Canada were treated, I feel a great sense of shame that Christians behaved in this way. Children were forcibly taken away from their parents and educated in Roman Catholic schools to learn to be Christians. They were often treated cruelly, and many died (Merasty, Time Magazine, 2022). It seems this use of force is not the way to achieve a universal religion. People need to come to it themselves through their own experience of God. It seems to me they can combine any new ideas with the ones they already have. It appears that all religions are paths to the same garden. We are all going to the same place ultimately, but we have different ways of getting there.

It was surprising to me that Hinduism was mentioned as being part of the true religion. The faith system is not something I knew a lot about though I realized it's incredibly ancient. I have come across some Hindu ideas in my practice of yoga. Meditation is a Hindu practice, and I have gained much by doing this each day. My mind is so much calmer than it used to be. I do believe that meditation has to be a major part of a universal religion. The origin of Hinduism is in the Vedas, which are ancient Sanskrit writings from India. Wisdom is passed down from spiritual teachers known as gurus. Hindus believe in reincarnation, as souls pass from one body to another according to the laws of karma. Hindus want to be liberated from the cycle of birth, death and rebirth and join with the Supreme being or Brahman. So God is like the world's soul. There is a great diversity in how God is worshipped in Hinduism. There is a proliferation of gods and goddesses. Three of the most important are Vishnu, Shiva and Shakti. Hindus worship in temples and at home (Hinduamerican.org, 2023). This brief research I have undertaken suggests Hinduism is similar to the spiritual world my guides are describing. There is a God who seems to be energy, so this fits in with the idea of the Supreme Being. My angels are also clear that reincarnation is a fact. So there's another similarity. I didn't meet any of the Hindu gods and goddesses, but my guides seem to be similar kinds of beings. Communion with the Divine through meditation is also vital in the explanation of my guides. Jesus spoke against idols, and he is clear that there is only one God. The other beings are angels or other spiritual entities.

Christianity does have the concept of an all-powerful God. This seems to fit with what my angels tell me and with Hinduism. In traditional Christianity, God is often depicted as an old man on a throne, but this image is metaphorical and does not fit with the truth of the spiritual world. Christianity grew out of Judaism because Jesus was a Jew. The Old Testament consists of Jewish writings about the history of the Jewish people. Christianity focuses on the life and death of Jesus Christ and his resurrection. The Bible is considered to be inspired by the Holy Spirit, and some Christians believe it is the literal word of God. Jesus Christ is the saviour of the world, and he is the promised Messiah that is talked about in Jewish scriptures. Through his crucifixion, Jesus paid the price for the sin of the world. Anyone who accepts the teaching of Christianity has eternal life, and their sins are forgiven. There will be a Judgement Day when Jesus will return to Earth to judge the living and the dead. He will then bring God's kingdom to Earth. Evil doers will go to Hell, and believers will dwell in Heaven. God consists of the Father, the Son and the Holy Spirit: the Trinity. Jesus is the Son of God and divine. He conquered death and was resurrected and appeared to his followers before ascending to Heaven. These days there are all kinds of Christian churches that have different beliefs (Lewis, 2012).

Some of the Christian beliefs differ from the information given to me by my angels. The all-powerful God seems to work. However, Christianity does not accept reincarnation as a belief.

There is only one life. My guides are adamant that there is no Hell. Everyone goes to Heaven regardless of their religion or what sins they have committed. My angels have not mentioned Judgement Day.

Malalia said we all live forever – we incarnate forever. She showed me an enormous bright light and said we all join with the light. So this is a departure from Christianity. In traditional Christian teaching, if we live a good life, we go to Heaven. Hell awaits for those who do evil. There is an idea that sin separates you from God. Atheists believe we just rot in the ground as we are just our bodies. Christianity has not accepted the idea of reincarnation. It is deep in the culture that we have one life, and we must do our best with it so that we go to Heaven.

Malalia was talking about being much more inclusive – *everyone* goes to the light. We all live forever – every single one of us. Even people who have done evil things. Even atheists go to the light. Everyone can also reincarnate. This is getting closer to a Buddhist or Hindu view of the world. The angels said, 'We can all do what Jesus did. We can raise ourselves. The secret is in Tibet. They know.' Malaysia told me to go to China. They would teach me, and I would teach them. We would learn from each other. She said that they would love me. I will find joy in Tibet. Everyone will know the truth. So it seems going to Tibet is an important part of my spiritual journey. I just need to figure out how to get there. When I asked. Jesus, he said walk. Well, that's a big ask. Walk to Tibet.

CHAPTER SEVEN:

Introducing Lucifer

One of my questions for my spirit guides was about religion. I had been on a spiritual path for a long time, and I had become a Christian. Christianity has helped me with my mental health. I found that it gave my life meaning. I enjoyed reading the Bible and saying the prayers. I found it hard to live up to the high ethical standards, but I was trying. Developing a personal relationship with Jesus brought me joy, and I now had a reason to go on living. I was still trying to figure out how to live a worthy Christian life. I liked going to my local church, but it was badly attended, so there were not many people to discuss my spiritual life with. Still, I felt lighter than I had in a long time.

However, I still had doubts about some aspects of the religion, and I wasn't sure about some of the teachings, like Hell and the Devil. I had always found the God of the Old Testament to be pretty scary, and He didn't seem to have much in common with the teachings of Jesus. God was presented as a being who was full of anger. In the story of Noah and the flood, He destroyed the whole Earth and only saved one family (Genesis 6:11-9:19). I was also horrified by the story of God telling Abraham to sacrifice his son Isaac (Genesis 22:1-19). Though the sacrifice did not take place, and an angel stepped in to save the boy, it is still hard to accept that God does this kind of thing. I felt close to Jesus and loved his message, but the Church always disappointed me in some ways. It seemed like a lot of the Church teaching was getting hung up on things that didn't really matter, and a lot of the people who go to Church do not seem particularly Christian in their way of life.

In Christianity, traditional Christians believe that Hell is a place that sinners go to after being judged. Hell is mentioned at points in the Old and New Testaments. The Book of Revelation

paints a particularly scary image with a lake of fire and burning sulphur and eternal torment for sinners (Revelation 20:10). We have all seen terrifying depictions of Hell in art like the paintings of Hieronymous Boschand the descriptions in Dante's *Inferno*. Generations of children have been terrified by these kinds of images. It seems hard to reconcile the idea of a loving God with the concept of Hell as a real place of eternal torment. Indeed, there seems to be great debate among different Christian sects as to the nature of Hell and whether it is a place or a state of being. Many modern Christians believe that those with faith in Jesus go to Heaven and atheists are annihilated. It turns out that a lot of the mentions of Hell in the Bible are mistranslations. In the Old Testament, the term Hell refers to the grave or tomb (Weiss, Jerusalem Post, 2021). In the New Testament, Jesus appears to refer to Hell, but we know that many people doctored his words for their own ends (Matthew 5:22, 29-30). In fact, the word he uses refers to a rubbish tip outside of Jerusalem, not a fiery place of eternal torment. Jesus is using this place as a metaphor. In the past, the Church has made use of the concept of Hell to control people. Some pastors are still doing that today. Jesus assures me in meditation that Hell does not exist. Everyone goes 'home' to what you might call Heaven or, as Michael Newton calls it, the place between lives.

I have also had trouble with the idea of the Devil. The Devil appears to be the personification of evil. I don't find it difficult to think of the concept of evil. I see people committing evil acts all around the world as I watch the horrors unfold on the news each night. The cruelty of war is a case in point. We have all heard of the supposed crimes inflicted on the civilian populations of Ukraine by invading soldiers. I have read stories about the Russians raping women, keeping civilians hostage, torture, and shooting people in the head. There have also been atrocities on the

Ukrainian side. In 2022, Russian forces in Bucha allegedly rounded up five men and executed one of them. They were forced to kneel by the side of the road and then one of them was shot in the back of the head. This was reported by an eyewitness (Schwartz, 2023). The Holocaust is another unspeakable evil that is difficult to comprehend. Between 1941 and 1945, six million Jewish people were murdered by the Nazis. The Nazis were attempting to kill all the Jews in Europe. Death squads in Eastern Europe and Russia killed Jews by firing squad. Then, concentration camps were created where many Jews were gassed in a systematic extermination (Holocaust Memorial Day Trust, 2023). Then we have seen the horrors that ISIS have inflicted on their enemies in the Middle East. ISIS stands for Islamic State in Iraq and Syria. The organisation aims to set up a caliphate in Iraq, Syria, and the surrounding countries. They wish to implement Sharia Law which is based on eighth-century Islam. In 2014, ISIS fighters attacked the Iraq town of Sinjar, home of a religious group called the Yazidis. According to a witness, 500 men were killed, and 70 children died of thirst. Women were sold into slavery (CNN.com, 2023). We can all think of countless horrors that human beings have inflicted on each other over the course of history.

There also seems to be a sense of evil just baked into the materialism of the world. Recently, I watched the awful scenes of the earthquakes in Turkey. This event seemed to be a natural disaster with no human cause. Yet so much suffering has come from it, with little children buried in the rubble. 50 000 people were killed and 100, 000 were injured (Redcross.org.uk, 2023). It is hard to understand how God lets this happen if God is an all-loving, all-powerful being.

People seem capable of evil acts, and there are evil events, but is there an actual Devil? In traditional Christianity, the Devil is a fallen angel who is the enemy of God. At the beginning of the world, it was perfect, and Adam and Eve, the first people, were sinless (Genesis 2:9). They disobeyed God, and there was a separation between people and God. The act of eating the apple from the Tree of Knowledge is called the original sin. The Devil is often referred to as Satan and can be depicted as a goat-headed man or a snake. It seems hard to believe that a loving God created the Devil to tempt humanity into sin, but that is what we are asked to believe in Christianity. There seems to be a contradiction within the Devil. The Devil does evil, but he has no free choice in this. If the Devil has no free choice, he cannot be held accountable for his actions. I did not understand this.

I was also drawn to Buddhism. I had learned to meditate at the Norwich Buddhist Centre and had some spiritual experiences through meditation. I had met with Jesus in deep meditation, and he appeared very clearly in my mind. He was a loving presence who comforted me. I had also had visions of my past lives in meditation and glimpses of possible futures. I had many visions of temples in Asia and Buddhist monks. I was attracted to Buddhism as a spiritual discipline, and I felt meditation was an aid to good mental health. I was also impressed with the joy that practitioners of Buddhism seemed to emanate. The emphasis on kindness and compassion appealed to me. Buddhism helps people to find peace within themselves. A daily practice of meditation helps people to develop kindness and wisdom, which they then share with others to benefit the world. The ultimate goal is the happiness of all living beings (Aboutbuddhism.org, 2023). Even so, I was bothered by the way the religion was described as atheistic with no loving God.

The various spiritual beliefs of the New Age had also held interest to me. I had dabbled with psychics and tarot cards but had found no fulfilment in these things. I think the idea of knowing the future appealed to me, particularly because I suffered from anxiety. I liked the way New Age beliefs were not as exclusive as the Church and seemed to be more welcoming to everyone. The beliefs seem to be wide-ranging and fluid. There appears to be acceptance of a Divine force which you could call God, which pervades everything. There are also angels and ascended masters who communicate with people through channelling or meditation.

There is often a belief in a lost civilization of the past, such as Atlantis or Lemuria. I had dabbled online with these things, but I felt some of the practitioners did not seem genuine, and I was worried about charlatans and deceivers. New Age seems to be just a term to describe a personal spirituality. I also worried that the New Age was a false light designed to draw people away from Christianity.

As not every religion could be wholly true, I was confused about all of this, and I wanted to know what form the afterlife would take, if any.

It was at this point in my session that a huge black angel appeared. His wing span was enormous, and as he walked towards me, I could see his face was like that of a goat, and he had horns on his head. He was wearing some kind of armour and dark cloth robes. I was pretty terrified of him, but he assured me he was not evil. To show me he meant me no harm, he knelt down in a gesture of taking the knee in front of me. It was the way a knight would kneel before a Queen. He introduced himself as Lucifer. This name means Light Bringer in Latin. He is also called the Morning Star, which is another name for the planet Venus. Venus appears as a bright star in the East just before sunrise, so that's how this name is applied to the planet. Jesus is also called the Morning Star in the Bible (Rev 22:16-17). Lucifer said he was not the Devil but just an angel. He stated that there was nothing to fear. He said that the Church made all the fearful things up. He told me that there were many evil people who were there at the setting up of Christianity as a Church and that there are evil people in the Vatican.

I had always been fascinated with Roman Catholicism, and I was tempted to convert to it from Anglicanism. My family, who originated in Ireland and then Scotland, were Roman Catholic at one point. Then they became communists. Lucifer's information made me realize that conversion was not a good idea. Of course, there are good people within the Roman Catholic Church, but also a lot of people doing the wrong thing. Lucifer did not enlarge on what he meant by evil people in the Vatican. He may have been referring to the widespread child abuse that we have all heard about. Not only is it bad enough that so many children have been sexually abused by priests, but also the way the Church leaders covered it up makes everything worse. A Vatican insider has estimated that up to a million Italian children have been abused over 70 years. One priest, John Joseph Geoghan, abused 130 boys over 34 years. The Archbishop of Boston covered it up, moving the priest between parishes. Such stories have been found across the world (Syed, 2022). I have heard other tales about the Vatican, such as corruption, fraud, money laundering and involvement with criminal elements (Posner, Forbes.com, 2021). There are also active homosexuals within the Vatican bureaucracy, even though this behaviour is condemned by the Church when it involves ordinary people. It has been suggested that eighty per cent of priests working in the Vatican are gay (Martel, 2019). I do believe God accepts and loves gay people, but the Vatican has chosen to be hypocritical about it. It is so sad that the original Church has fallen so far from the message of Jesus. It is no wonder that Church attendance is so low.

It seems that the founders of the Christian Church changed a lot of elements from the original teachings of Jesus. Jesus did not have a church but taught people out in the open places. After his death, the early Christians often met in synagogues, as many of them were Jewish. St. Paul set up churches throughout the Roman Empire. Christians were often persecuted by the Romans. The Emperor Nero had Christians arrested and tortured. They were torn to death by dogs, crucified and set on fire. In spite of this early opposition, the Emperor Constantine became a Christian in 312 AD (Request.org.uk, 2023). It has been suggested that Constantine kept up his pagan beliefs alongside his Christianity. He may have felt the Christian God would enhance his power and give him victory in battle. None of this accords well with the peaceful teachings of Jesus. Constantine carried out some evil acts in his lifetime. He had his son Crispus poisoned, and he ordered his wife Fausta to be killed in a hot bath (Goldsworthy, 2010). Christianity became the religion of the Roman Empire and spread across the world.

The structure and hierarchy with bishops, archbishops and a supposedly infallible Pope does not seem to sit well with the preaching of equality by the simple, humble Jesus: "Very truly I tell you, no servant is greater than his master, nor is a messenger greater than the one who sent them." (John 13:16).

St. Paul had much to do with the setting up of the early churches, and you can read about his exploits in the New Testament. St. Paul has had a great influence on the teachings and beliefs of the Christian Church. It seems to me that a lot of this is Paul's own interpretation rather than the words and views of Jesus himself. His views on women have meant that the female sex has been denied leadership roles in the Church until recent times (1 Timothy 2:9-15). Some have argued that Paul deliberately corrupted the teachings of Jesus, introducing some pagan elements, over-emphasising the role of the crucifixion and introducing original sin and the need for redemption. Paul also is responsible for the doctrine of the Trinity: the Father, the Son and the Holy Spirit that Muslim scholars disagree with (Landau-Tasseron, 1990). It seems to me that Lucifer is correct in stating that the early Church corrupted the original words of Jesus for its own selfish purposes.

Lucifer said that he was a fallen angel. He fell to Earth. He said, 'You fell, we fell. We all fell down. Lots of us fell.' He said we were Nephilim: a race of angelic beings. Now we are mixed in with humans. I noticed that he used the word 'we', implying that I had also fallen with him as had other spiritual beings. He said that we all fell. I believe he is using this falling as a metaphor to explain the origins of the human race. The DNA of a more evolved species of aliens was mixed in with the original primitive beings who were inhabiting the Earth. The combination gives rise to humans as we know them today. We are all aliens or angels, whatever name you prefer. We are spiritual beings encased in ape-like material bodies.

The purpose of falling was to bring human beings to the light. This explanation is different to that of the Church. Lucifer was not sent to Earth by God as a punishment. He volunteered to come to help the human race. He brought knowledge. This is why he is referred to as the Light Bringer. While he was explaining about falling, I could see lots of lights falling onto the earth like a meteor shower. The word Nephilim appears in the Old Testament in the Book of Genesis. They are referred to as giants and mighty men (Genesis 6:4). The Nephilim are the offspring of angels and human women. The story in Genesis seems to be a version of what Lucifer told me. In Hebrew, the word Nephilim literally translates as the fallen ones, which seems to fit with what Lucifer said. In most Christian interpretations, the Nephilim are considered to be evil, and God sent the flood to destroy them. Some scholars believe that the Nephilim were banished to Hell, but others say they remained on the Earth as demons to lead people astray. This is not the interpretation that Lucifer gave me. According to Lucifer, the Nephilim were a race of angelic beings who came to help mankind.

Lucifer explained that Jesus is not the same as him. Jesus was a man, not an angel. Lucifer and Malalia are not human. They have never lived on Earth as people. Lucifer lives on Earth as an angel. It is hard for me to understand exactly how he does this. It's like he presides over the Earth as his domain. He does not lead people astray or tempt people. Human beings have free will, so they can choose to do good or evil. If we all become more aware of the spirit within us, we are more likely to do good in the world. It's as if there is a spiritual battle going on within each of us. We need to get in touch with our spiritual angelic nature and defeat the material animal brain, which can lead us into evil. The body wants to satisfy itself with sensual delights. Too much emphasis on the material plane leads us into trouble. We can tame the senses and tame the mind through meditation. Continual practice of meditation brings us peace of mind. We are then at ease with ourselves and can feel compassion for others. All around me, I see people obsessed with the acquisition of money so they can satisfy their senses. It seems to me that the seeking of sensual satisfaction does not make anyone happy. I have a neighbour who drives a luxury sports car. The car costs more than most people's houses. I have to say I have yet to see him smile. He rarely leaves his house when he is not working and does not interact with anyone in the village. I doubt he has achieved real happiness.

I channelled Lucifer on a later occasion in response to a question from another writer. This is what he said. I am Lucifer. The Light Bringer. The Morning Star. I am an Archangel. I fell down to Earth as the Elohim. We were called the Nephilim. We came to help humanity – to give knowledge. I did not incarnate as a person. I am and have always been an archangel, and I always will be. I volunteered to preside over the Earth for God. Here we are apart from God. It is the plan. We are in a game or an illusion. We have free will on Earth. We need to choose the Light – do good acts. We are not prevented from doing evil. There has been so much wrong written about me. I am part of the Light. I do not ask for blood. Those who sacrifice to me are mistaken. I am very sad. It's hard to be away from God. I am sad that the Church has twisted what I am. I came from Venus. I am one of the Eloha. We are high spiritual beings. Eventually, everyone will come back to the Light. Then I can also return to the Light. I am full of love for humanity. I will help you if you ask me. I am on Earth. I am everywhere. Hell does not exist. Earth is the closest to Hell that we have. I have nothing to do with demons. I am not in charge of them. The mistake of the Church refers to misunderstanding the verse in

Isaiah (Isaiah 14:12). He was referring to the King of Babylon, not me. God sent me. I did not rebel against God. Humanity's task is to return to God – to choose light. It takes thousands of years. This is enough. End of transmission.

Jesus came to Earth to show people how they should live, but it's all gone wrong. The Church has changed so much of Jesus' message that it is all messed up now. The core teaching was that through love, we raise ourselves. It's like you know the truth all along, then you forget it and learn it again. We slowly come back to God. I need to trust myself that I know the truth. I already know what is right and wrong. My guides used the image from the film The Wizard of Oz (Warnerbros.co.uk, 2023). They said that I had always had the red shoes. It was funny because The Wizard of Oz was always one of my favourite films. Dorothy lives on a farm in Kansas, but she has a bump on the head and goes to the magical Land of Oz. All the time, she keeps telling everyone that she wants to go home, but she doesn't know how to get there. She even goes to see the wizard to ask for help, but she can't get home no matter what she does. Then she is told that all she had to do was to tap her red shoes together and she could be home any time she wanted. This is such a good metaphor for how it is to be human. We have a yearning to go home to Heaven, but we don't know how to get there. We try all kinds of religions and practices, but none of them seem to help. The truth is that Heaven is inside of us all the time.

We can go there whenever we want through meditation. It's like we have an inner sense of what is right and wrong and what is true deep inside of us, but we give our power away to priests, psychics or politicians and let them decide what is best for us. We need to trust ourselves that we know the truth for ourselves. If we could all come to see this, there would be a spiritual awakening on Earth. We need to realize that we are spiritual beings having a human experience. We all have a spark of the Divine light inside of us. It is our earthly bodies that are leading us astray rather than Lucifer or the Devil. Our divine souls are eternal, beautiful and good. They choose to incarnate into a human body to have an experience of separation from God. The human body evolved from animals, from a kind of ape, so it has animal instincts. Deep inside the human brain, the amygdala is trying to keep us safe. It fills us full of fear so that we stay alive. This is fine when we are fleeing from a tiger, but in spiritual terms, it is holding us back. It is important not to be afraid but to trust God. Fear stops us from fully realizing our spiritual selves. Look at the way most of us behave. We spend our lives seeking security by amassing money and making a safe home to hide out in. We love to assuage our physical needs by eating delicious foods, having sex and drinking. We spend our evenings entertaining our brains with television and computer games. All of these things are just appealing to our bodily urges, the animal part of ourselves. Most of us may feel dissatisfied with our lives for much of the time, no matter how much money we have or how many cuisines we can enjoy. This is because we are denying our spiritual side, the soul deep within us, which is yearning to be heard. The soul finds it easier to communicate with us when we dial down the physical pleasures. We can see how people in the past have achieved this when we look at the lives of the saints.

I have always loved the story of St Francis. He was an Italian monk who founded the Franciscan order. He lived an ascetic life of poverty in his later years though he had been wealthy as a young man. He spent time in lonely places where he had visions of Jesus, who told him to rebuild the Church. Just like St Francis, we can have mystical experiences by denying our bodily urges and living simply. Being alone in quiet places is a way of getting in touch with the Divine. St Francis was trying to live as Jesus did. He preached to ordinary people and even to animals. St Francis had his mystical visions when he was fasting. It seems that if we stop paying so much attention to the body, we can join with God and the angels (Morgan Cron, 2013).

All the knowledge I need is inside me. I just have to be confident in myself that I know. Everyone needs to come together. There needs to be a new spiritual message. All religions can join together. Everybody knows the truth, but they have forgotten.

They need to go inside themselves, and then they will remember. I need to teach them to go inside – to meditate. This is an important part of my life purpose. I need to bring the light to people by telling them that it is inside of them. We don't need an organized religion but a personal spirituality that we see for ourselves. People need to be empowered to know that they can come to the light without looking for external saviours. It's time for a new promise or a New Testament. We can all join with God through meditation.

It seems daunting to set up a new spirituality for the whole world. Each of us must wake up and then tell others how to do it. A Google search tells me that there are many people who have received similar information. Lots of people refer to themselves as star seeds and believe they have come from other planets to help the people of Earth. If we all join together, we can lead people back to the light. In fact, all of us are spiritual beings. We just don't realize it.

Richard Martini, a film director and journalist, has been filming and writing about people's encounters with spiritual beings via mediums or hypnotherapists or just through guided

meditations. Jesus has featured many times in these sessions, as have other spiritual masters and deceased people (Martini, 2023). There is also a website called Channelling Erik and a YouTube channel where Elisa Medhus communicates with spiritual beings and the deceased with the help of her dead son Erik. She has many talented mediums and psychics as guests, and they seem to be relaying similar information to that which I am receiving (Channelingerik.com, 2023). It seems we are already building a community of people who are waking up.

CHAPTER EIGHT:

Life Purpose

My life purpose is to write about the light. I have been trying to write but have found it very slow. I have written two novels, but they weren't accepted for publication which disheartened me. I self-published them on Amazon, but not many people have read them. I have been procrastinating a lot and have not been very productive in recent years. Writing about the light gives me a new perspective to help inspire my writing. I hope to help people through my work. I always wanted to be a writer when I was a child, and I used to get praise for my creative work at school. I remember winning the Easter poetry prize many times. Somehow, it fell by the wayside as I concentrated on my career, and I lost belief that I could do it. It's time for that to change now. Through my words, I want others to awaken to their true spiritual nature. In this way, I can truly help people. If you find the spiritual side of yourself, life becomes so much easier. You realize that you are an eternal spiritual being.

This life is just like a show or a game. We are in a gigantic theatre production. None of it is real. The ultimate reality is in another dimension. Once you start to trust God and yourself, you can free your mind from depression, anxiety and all the other problems that beset so many of us.

My guides told me to free myself from heaviness. I need to feel joy and let it all go. I must slough off all darkness. They told me to leave it all behind. I must laugh and be joyful. It is important to leave the darkness behind and listen to my guides. I have always had a tendency to depression, over-thinking and lack of confidence. These are all things I am working on to get rid of. I need to do much more meditation and find a way of life that gives me joy. Writing is a way of doing joyful work.

I need to get in the flow. Flow is a word you read a lot in spiritual writings. If you are in the flow or in the zone, you are fully immersed in an activity with a mental state of energized focus. I think I was much better at this as a child than I am now. If you pause to watch children playing, you can see how they are in flow, absorbed fully with the imaginary world they have created. I want to be able to feel in flow when I am writing. If I am in the flow, I am concentrating on the present moment. Action and awareness melt together, and I lose the sense of myself as an individual ego. I feel rewarded by the action of writing and lose all sense of time.

I have spent far too much time being distracted so that my attention is all over the place. Meditation helps with achieving the state of flow.

My guides tell me I can achieve a flow state through travelling. I must go to the holy places and the high places. I remember when I lived in the Highlands of Scotland near Oban; I felt much more spiritual than I normally do. There are many 'thin' places in the world where the veil between the worlds seems to have melted away to some extent. I have also felt this on mountains and on islands. It is possible to feel it in some churches or temples, but not always. My guides showed me images of walking and travelling over seas and oceans. I would love to travel more, but I worry about having the finances to do it. I need to think of a way. I know in India and parts of the East, there is a tradition of wandering holy men who beg for what they need. I think this is the kind of movement my guides have in mind. It is alien to us in the West, where beggars are usually looked down on as alcoholics or drug addicts rather than holy people. It takes a whole lot of faith in God to just step out of the door with nothing. I think it could be incredibly healing, though. I have often felt anxious about travelling alone. Women can feel vulnerable to predatory men, and there is the danger of robbery and injury. I must overcome this sense of anxiety about being alone.

I have been working as a hypnotherapist, and they said this was one way of telling people about the light but writing a book is better as you can reach more people more quickly. Jesus told me to write about the light. It became apparent that Jesus didn't think much of hypnotherapy. He approved of past life regression and the Life Between Lives sessions designed by Michael Newton, but he felt that a lot of hypnotherapy was not focusing on the right things. He liked the work of Scott de Tamble. If people spent time getting their spiritual life into order, they wouldn't need to bother with the stop smoking, lose weight and other issues that most hypnotherapists deal with. He did feel that hypnotherapy is full of charlatans and hucksters, so its reputation has been ruined. Sadly, I have found this to be true myself, and I have had my fingers burned a few times by unethical practitioners. Jesus said it was better to talk to your guides directly about your problems rather than to go to a hypnotherapist. He felt that hypnotherapy was too slow a method and it had been corrupted by dark people. The problem is how people see hypnosis and the way most therapists do it. I can reach more people with writing. It's better to obtain information straight from the source. At this point, my guides put a picture of a huge ball of light in my head as an image representing the Source. They said it was too much to talk to God directly but that the correct information could come through the guides. So my mission was to write about the light. You can find out your life purpose by communicating with your guides.

Another question I had was about money. I had struggled with money all my life. I had grown up in modest circumstances where there never seemed to be enough money. I think I developed an inferiority complex in childhood because all my friends seemed to have more money than me. I vowed to be rich when I grew up, but this didn't happen either. I became a teacher but struggled a lot with managing my income. It just seemed to disappear, and I found it hard to save. I am ashamed to say I have frittered lots of money away on eating out, clothes, concerts, and holidays. I was trying to fulfil my senses and neglecting my true spiritual nature. None of it made me happy. I was always walking out of jobs due to people bullying me. Then I would get a new one, and the same thing would happen again. Now I had a hypnotherapy business, but I didn't get enough clients to make a decent amount of money. I had also written two novels, but they hadn't sold much. I was beginning to think I was jinxed. So I was in desperate need of financial advice from my guides.

My guides said to trust, and it will come. People will come to help me. I need to believe that it is possible. I should travel and write. They said that they would always take care of me. They reminded me that I had never been hungry in my life. This is true.

As a privileged Western person, I have always had enough to eat, clothes and a roof over my head though I have never been rich. It's humbling to think that there are so many people in the world who are homeless and starving. In comparison to them, I am rich indeed. The guides reminded me not to get caught up in distractions. They will send help to me. Other people have money as it comes easily to them, and they can support me. I should just flow with it. Just believe.

The guides went on to talk about manifestation. You can make money with your mind. It's important to focus on the good, not the lack. Just do what you love. Money is not the goal but the by-product. I have not managed to be good at manifesting things yet, but I am working on it. The angels put the name of Bruce Lipton into my head. He has lots of videos available for free about manifestation. He has also written books on the subject, one of which has sold many copies explaining how our thoughts affect our reality (Lipton, 2010).

Manifestation is a form of energy manipulation that you can learn. When I read the Bible, I see Jesus doing this when he turns the water into wine (John 2:1-11) and when he creates the loaves and fishes to feed a crowd (Matthew 14:17-19).

I can have what I want. It seemed like money wasn't very important to the spirit guides. Of course, they don't have to live on the Earth. They don't need to eat or pay their bills. They said you act like money is already there when you have an abundance mindset. People can teach you to have an abundance of consciousness. Just open yourself to abundance and meditate on it.

The guides told me to forget the past. People have tried to bring me down so many times. There has been lots of belittling of me. Other people have discouraged me. I often have memories in my head of people saying nasty things. It seems like the world is full of toxic people. They can't do things they want, so they drag others down. I have felt a target of this kind of bullying so many times. There is a sickness deep within our society. If people were happy and in touch with their divinity, they wouldn't feel the need to say mean things to others. I need to shield myself from them. I have always wanted to live by the sea and write novels. That is one path I can take.

Scott asked the guides about my chronic fatigue. I have had this for years. I lack energy, and I have to force myself to do things. They said it was caused by sadness from the past. The weight of the earth is so heavy. It pulls me down. I need to rise above it. I must remember that I am divine and that I am part of the light. Let it all go.

There has been much darkness in my past. Some people have been mean to me. There has not been much love. People have disappointed me. There has been so much harshness and cruelty with words. This is the punitive nature of people. My parents were harsh people and not demonstrative. I don't think they were capable of loving me. Maybe I was strange to them.

My sister enjoyed being unkind to me. At school, there were many unpleasant people, particularly when I went to senior school at age eleven. It was as if people had lost their childhood innocence and discovered the dark side of their natures. In the workplace, I was disappointed to find the same patterns. So many unsealed people were saying nasty things to me, trying to get me into trouble and generally being unpleasant to be around. Of course, I did meet good people, but it was as if they were outnumbered by the dark people. The guides said I was not to focus on these people but to lift myself up. My life has been a test: Can you come back to the light when you have seen the darkness? Yes, you can. I have.

I am to focus on myself and my spirit guides. They said they had put me in darkness so I can come back to the light. I trusted people who weren't worthy of my trust. People are not capable of unconditional love. The guides are. I am one of them, so I could never understand people. Now I do.

Scott asked me about education. The guides said I had enough conventional education. I actually have three degrees: one in Philosophy, one in Psychology and a Masters in Psychology. I have always enjoyed studying. It's strange how all this learning has never seemed to help me to be successful in the workplace. I now need to learn more about the spiritual. I should learn in the temple. I am not sure which temple they are referring to. Maybe it is a Buddhist temple. The guides also use the word temple to mean the heart. So again I need to go within myself and meditate on my heart space. In this way, I can focus on love.

CHAPTER NINE:

Dealing with Depression and Anxiety

I have struggled with depression and anxiety many times in my life. I was an extremely shy child, which is just a form of social anxiety. In later childhood, I developed depression, which was undiagnosed. I think I always felt different to other people, and I didn't fit in. I didn't feel much love from my family, and I felt they didn't really want me or like me. At primary school, I had friends, and I thought I was reasonably popular. In secondary school, I felt like everyone had fallen away, and I had no friends outside of school. My school was a rough, harsh place, and there was lots of bullying and unkindness towards many people. I lost myself in books. My weekly riding lesson was a highlight of my week. In fact, it was the only highlight. At university, I felt normal for a while, but as boyfriends kept dumping me, I took solace in alcohol and music. When I started work, I put on a front of confidence and became loud, funny and lively. This persona didn't work either as lots of staff members seemed to take a dislike to me. I had ups and downs relating to success at work, but mostly, I felt I wasn't good enough. The meanness and harshness of my school days seemed to follow me into the staff rooms. Teaching had a lot of dysfunctional people within it who like nothing better than to take their insecurities out on others.

When I finally left teaching, my anxiety and depression hit me with full force. There was a time in my life when I didn't get out of bed for days. I would sleep and drink wine and then go back to bed. I just felt like I had given life my best shot, but I had failed utterly. I had been bullied out of the only career I knew by some deeply unpleasant managers. I remember once my final headteacher once asked me how I had got through teaching practice. He said this in a room full of people. I was working so hard at that school and doing my best for the children. This unpleasant man seemed to enjoy being unkind to me for some reason I did not understand. He seemed to prefer men and gave the male staff all the promotions and opportunities while the women were ignored. I felt I had given my all but had been thwarted at every turn. I accepted that teaching in the English school system was not the right path for me.

Scott asked the guides about this time in my life. They said that it was a test. I had allowed people to hurt me. I should not set too much store by their view of the world. They were in the wrong, not me. There are many people who have wanted to destroy me over the years. They don't understand me. The guides said it was their own darkness that made them do it. They hate themselves, so they want to bring me down to their level. I am not to care about what people think. Jesus used a line from the Bible: 'Render to Caesar what is Caesar's and to God what is God's' (Mark 12:17). People are of this world, and they have their rules and their ways of doing things. The Divine is more important than the human world. I should focus on the world beyond. I don't need to follow human rules. I felt such love from my guides over this dark time in my life. They were so understanding and not judgmental about the things I had done wrong.

The guides were clear that human institutions are all rotten. This corruption is evident in the Church, in government, in health, and in education. The divine love is missing. Our society has lost touch with spirituality. Every day I read about some scandal involving politicians. One example is so many of them lie about their expenses so that they can obtain more money for themselves. One of them even claimed for money to heat his horses' stables. Amazingly, this person is still in politics (The Guardian, 2013). So many people are just thinking about their own enrichment rather than helping others. The idea of selfless public service seems to have died. Recently, with the Covid-19 pandemic, many people were seeing it as an opportunity to make money rather than solve the problem. It seems we have been duped into taking vaccines that many of us did not need (Vogel, 2021). Spirituality has been lost. In my therapy work, I find the people who need my help the most cannot afford to pay for it. The health service only offers brief cognitive behavioural therapy that does not work for many people. Education has lost its way with a focus on targets and levels. Teachers are constantly judged by inspectors and found wanting. Recently, a headteacher committed suicide after being found inadequate by the inspection system (Sinmaz, 2023). It is all totally demoralizing. Schools have lost focus on what is truly important. My guides tell me that my solution is to find freedom. I must let everything go and travel alone into the world. I am not sure how this is possible at this point, but I am figuring it out.

My purpose is to become one with God and everything that is: oneness. This is the same purpose for everyone. We all need to discover our spiritual nature. Oneness is becoming the entire universe. It is a state of pure joy and bliss. There is no sense of time. There is peace, harmony and unbounded love. It is hard for human beings to achieve this state though we can read about it in the lives of the saints and mystics (Ramirez, 2016). It is also apparent in some Buddhist monks and other sages (Suzuki, 1957). We need to transcend the mind and the ego. Everything is connected, so you are always connected to God. You just don't realize it. Here on Earth, we are having an experience of separation, but we can rediscover unity through meditation. We might have had glimpses of oneness at certain times in our life. You may have been watching a sunset and had a feeling of immense joy just knowing that you are a part of the universe. Maybe you looked at your child and felt a oneness with all beings.

Being in nature, just watching birds in your garden can give you joy and peace. For most of us, these experiences are fleeting. It is possible to live in this state of oneness all of the time. I am a long way off at the moment.

My gift is communication, so my guides tell me. I am the bridge between the spiritual world and the world of men. I stand between. I must tell people what the guides say. I must spread the light. The book you are reading is an attempt to do that.

There are three Venusians currently on the Earth, and we are to come together for a divine mission. One of them I had already met. I had a massive crush on him at university, but we didn't have a relationship. Later, we reconnected briefly, but we didn't keep up the friendship. The other one was shown to me as a Tibetan that I hadn't met yet. We are all supposed to come together in China. Currently, my old friend has not returned to the light, but someone is trying to help him to do this. There is nothing I can do about it.

CHAPTER TEN:

Venus – the Home World

Scott, my therapist, suggested that I spend some time in the home world as this could benefit me in my current life. I had already been told that my original world was the planet Venus, but not the physical planet. Rather, Venus is another dimension where you don't need a physical body.

The planet Venus has always held importance for human beings. It is known as the Morning Star and the Evening Star, as it appears as the brightest star in the sky just before sunrise and after sunset. It is the second planet from the sun in our solar system. Today, the planet is uninhabitable. The surface of Venus is unbearably hot, and the atmosphere consists of carbon dioxide. It cannot support human life. In the dim and distant past, it had oceans and a more livable climate (Simon, 2012). The name Venus derives from the Roman goddess of Love and Beauty. She emerged fully formed from the sea in ancient times to teach humanity about love. In a meditation session, I had a vision of Venus coming out of the waves. She was a huge giant and was wearing a short leather tunic and carrying a dagger. There were people in boats on the sea rowing away from her in terror. The path that Venus takes as it is seen from the Earth is like a pentagram. It has also been compared to a rose. Interestingly, there are lines on my left hand that make the shape of a pentagram.

There is a spiritual planet Venus which is not in the physical plane. This is where the alien Venusians live. They have evolved so much that they are no longer physical. They have what

we might call light bodies. They have appeared to people on Earth as angels or aliens. They can incarnate in human form, and they do this to bring wisdom to human beings. Venusians have been great spiritual teachers such as Jesus, Buddha and Confucius. In astrology, Venus is often associated with the Divine Feminine. It relates to the body, beauty, love, relationships and abundance. Venus is also a healing energy and uplifts us to a higher vibrational level.

I had the sensation of being on a spaceship. I was sitting and felt surrounded by strong vibrations. I could feel myself being jolted, and I was finding it difficult to hold myself in place. It was as if we were moving at an incredible speed, a little like when you take off in an aircraft. I noticed an incredible number of colours all around me, like candy stripes. We were moving through space and time. Eventually, we arrived on Venus.

I was sitting on a long couch outside a building that looked like a kind of palace. There were white marble columns all around me, as you see in Ancient Greek scenes. I was with other Venusians, and we were sitting looking up at the stars. It was serene, and the place felt full of love. Everything seemed elegant and beautifully done. We were just chatting with each other, totally at ease. The buildings were open to the skies. Venusians have no need for sleep, so they don't need beds. We don't need to eat or procreate. I felt I knew the other beings I was sitting with very well. There was a sense of total harmony between us. We all understood each other completely. We enjoyed watching over other less advanced races and helping them. We chose, at times to incarnate on Earth. This human experience helped our own development and also helped the people of that planet. We also incarnate on other planets. Our intentions are good. We have been worried about the Earth because of nuclear weapons. There have been many times in the past when we have prevented nuclear war. Sometimes, we travel to the silos and neutralize the weapons so that they cannot be fired. The Earth people keep going off on the wrong track and need to be brought back into balance. We don't think humans are ready to deal with the power of nuclear energy. We have approached world leaders in the past to ask them to give up their weapons, but they would not.

I was then shown scenes of other Venusians. They actually looked like translucent aliens. They had large heads and thin arms and legs, and they were smaller than the average person. Their bodies seemed to shimmer and be full of light. In an instant, they could appear differently. They can look human or, indeed, like anything they want. The Venusians communicate through telepathy. They are spiritual beings who do not have physical bodies. They just appear to be physical to us, so we can see them. Venusians have appeared many times to people on our planet and often show themselves as tall blonde people like you would see in a place like Sweden.

On Scott's suggestion, I came back from Venus to Earth. Instantly, I felt a heaviness and a darkness descend on me. It felt so much easier to live on Venus.

CHAPTER ELEVEN:

The Spirit Council Speaks

At Scott's suggestion, the rest of my Spirit Council were encouraged to talk to me. The first to come forward was the Chinese Sage. He was dressed in beautifully coloured silk robes, and he had a little velvet black hat on his head. His beard was long, and he had his arms folded in front of him. He seemed old and wise. His message to me was to learn more about Buddhism and Confucianism. It was particularly important for people to show compassion to each other. He told me that Buddhism, at its core, had the same message as Christianity.

Buddhism has its origins in India in the fifth century BCE. Its aim is to liberate people from their earthly suffering. Suffering is caused by being too attached to the material world. The teaching emphasizes a middle way. People should not be too ascetic in their lifestyles, but also they should not be too hedonistic. Buddhists train their minds through meditation. The ultimate goal is to escape the continual cycle of reincarnation and achieve enlightenment. It is important for all beings to be helped to achieve this aim.

Buddha was born as Siddhartha in Nepal. He wanted to relieve people's suffering on Earth and set about learning meditation. He began to live an extremely ascetic lifestyle. He fasted for much of the time, meditated and employed breathwork techniques. During meditation under the Bodhi tree, he was given wisdom: the right way to live is the middle way. One must not be too self-denying nor too loving of pleasure. We must not cling to the material world, which only brings us suffering. People are reborn into good or bad circumstances according to their karma or the good or bad deeds, they have done in their previous lives. Nirvana is reached when the cycle of suffering ends. The person can then live in a state of bliss. Many followers of Buddhism choose to live in monastic communities. It is important to have a kind attitude to all living beings (Dalai Lama, 2009). Jesus had already told me that Buddhism has a lot of the truth of the spiritual reality of the world but not the whole truth.

The guide showed me images of me travelling to the East on horseback. We seemed to be on little grey ponies, and I was in a line with lots of other people. We were riding through hilly country and up mountainsides. It was China. Eventually, we came to a great ancient city. It was Lhasa in Tibet. The sage told me that everything I needed was here in Lhasa. They would teach me in the temple. I can go in life, but I can also travel there in dreams. Lhasa has immense spiritual power. Meditation can tell me everything I need to know.

Tibet has long held a fascination for me, and I have wanted to go there for as long as I can remember. It seems there is some secret knowledge there that I need to find out about. Currently, it is impossible to travel independently to Tibet as it is now part of China. One needs to go as a member of an official guided group. Tibet is the highest country on Earth. It seemed to flourish in the seventh century when Tibet had a great empire (Lioy, 2019). My guides tell me that Jesus visited the area in his youth. At this time, Tibet was not a unified kingdom. Many people practised an ancient religion that preceded Buddhism. The people received teaching from a spiritual being who taught them how to free themselves from the wheel of karma. Buddhism spread in Tibet from the seventh century onwards. Some Tibetans were practising the Bon religion, which is similar to Buddhism (Rossi, 2000). There is a belief in local deities. At the time that Jesus visited, there was also a shamanic nature religion still in existence. Places were full of their own gods and demons. Spirits inhabited the natural world.

There is a story that Jesus visited and studied at a monastery in Hemis in his youth. Hemis is now in India, but it used to be part of Tibet. A Russian journalist called Nicolas Notovitch visited Hemis and talked to the Llama there, who gave him a document which he had translated. This document was called *The Life of Saint Issa, Best of the Sons of Men,* and was an account of Jesus' travels in the East. Notovitch wrote a book about his time in the monastery (Notovitch, 1894). Some scholars believe that Notovitch made up this story, and the original document is now lost. Tibetans are a deeply spiritual people, and the land appears to be infused with spiritual power. It is one of the 'thin' places where the veil between the worlds is narrow. I have experienced this feeling in the West Highlands of Scotland. Most of the places we live are too busy to feel it.

Lhasa is the capital city of Tibet. Its name literally means place of the gods. Lhasa sits in the centre of the Tibetan Plateau. I am supposed to find a document there which has been lost to Western scholarship but has great importance. I wonder if this is the Kanjar of Hemis which Notovitch wrote about. Many documents were destroyed by the Chinese invasion of Tibet, but nowadays there is a project to document all of the scrolls in the Potala Palace in Lhasa by Chinese academics (Chan, 2023). Perhaps the document will be found here. There are thousands of documents made with gold, silver and turquoise on materials like wood, brocade and patta leaves.

The next guide to speak was the African Shaman. He was a dark-skinned man with short hair and a thin body. He was wearing a short, red robe, and he had a wooden staff in his hand. He told me that the most important message was love. He said that love joins everything together. He told me that shamanism was a great thing to learn. It was a doorway into the spirit world. It was a different way into the methods I had been using. He told me that all the world's belief systems should be joined together into one religion.

Shamanistic belief systems were the indigenous religions of Africa. Nowadays, many Africans follow Christianity or Islam. There is a great diversity of belief in shamanistic religions, and spirituality is tied to particular places. The spiritual life is not separate from the mundane everyday activities. Shamanistic religions are holistic. If you are sick, it is not just a problem with your body. There is also a problem with your social life and with your ancestors. Ancestors still play a role in the life of the living. Many African belief systems conceive of a supreme creator being and other deities. There is no written text, and the traditions are passed on orally. African religions are happy to mix elements of

Christianity and Islam into their practices. This fits well with what my angels are telling me to do.

African shamans can be thought of as holy men. They are healers and commune with spirits. Honouring these spirits keeps the community safe from misfortune. It is possible to train to become an African shaman. John Lockley spent ten years in apprenticeship with MaMngwevu, a medicine woman from the Xhosa tribe in South Africa. He now teaches all over the world (Lockley, 2017). Shamanism is something I would love to learn.

Next, Mother Mary came forward. Though she didn't introduce herself by name, I had a strong feeling that she was the mother of Jesus. She had long, dark hair, and her head was partly covered with a blue veil like a nun would wear. She called herself the Mother. Her energy was amazing. I could feel so much pure love emanating from her, and she made me feel so at ease and peaceful. She gave me a warm hug, and I felt like I just wanted to stay there forever. She told me to trust the spirit guides. Everything was going to be ok. She said, 'We love you.' Everything is fine. She was nothing like the cold, white statues you see in shrines. It is funny to me that the Roman Catholic Church is so formal in its services and prayers that honour Mary, and yet she seemed nothing like this in person. Just like Jesus, she does not want people to be so stiff with her. She has a simple message of love.

The final spirit guide to come forward was one I hadn't noticed before. He was Anubis, the Egyptian god. He didn't introduce himself, and I only learned who he was later. He had the body of a man, and he was wearing a short tunic. His head was covered with a striped material, so I could not see his face. I had the distinct impression that he didn't want to show it to me in case he frightened me. Anubis is half man and half jackal. He told me he was worshipped as a god in Egypt a long time ago. He was clear that he was not a god, but he was a spiritual being, not human. He told me that I was stronger than I thought. He encouraged me to touch his chest so I could take some of his strength. He felt incredibly strong, fierce and powerful. I was to be strong like a lion.

The ancient Egyptians considered Anubis the god of funerals and graves, and he was a guide to the underworld. He knew how to embalm bodies. He was present when people died, and were judged in the afterlife. There was a weighing of the heart ceremony where a person was judged on their deeds to see if they were fit to go into the afterlife. Anubis does not want to be worshipped, but he is available to talk to and to give advice.

Malalia came forward again. She told me that the spirits are always around me, and they communicate with me through telepathy. She said that there was so much beauty to come. I needed to keep going, to keep coming back to them.

Scott asked if we could see God, but Malalia was reluctant. She said it was too powerful and it would blow your mind. I am not ready to see God yet. They gave me a glimpse of what God is. He is everything that is, but it's too powerful to see. I just need to know that it's there and not be afraid. God showed Himself to me in the form of a lion. He was roaring fiercely and came out of a white cloud that was like a ball of energy. This was a metaphor to explain spiritual power to me rather than what He actually looks like. At one point, it was like I became one with Him. I could feel the energy flowing through me as if there was a force moving through my veins and all parts of my body. Everything was pulsating together like some kind of amazing symphony. Everything was melting into everything else. You are in me, and I am in you. This is also the same for everyone else. We all come together in unity. I then came back into myself again, and I could just see a roaring lion again.

Malalia finished the session by telling me I know everything I need to know. All is inside me. I can have everything I want if I believe. I need to turn off the conscious part of the brain. This kind of communication with guides is not rational. I need to stop blocking it. Then I can flow with the universe. Just be. I am ready now. Just open to love. Keep opening.

All is as it should be.

Then Scott counted me back to full awareness, and I was back in my study in Norfolk, England, thinking that I had just had the most incredible experience of my life.

CHAPTER TWELVE:

Reflections

I shared my session even though it's personal to me because I think the truths within it apply to everyone on Earth. In this chapter, I want to elaborate on what I think these truths are and how they can help people.

Jesus told me that his core teaching was through love, we raise ourselves. So what does this actually mean? There is only one word for love in English, so the word has to do a lot of heavy lifting. I listened to so many pop songs as a child talking about love that I came to believe it only concerned romantic or erotic love. I looked for this love from men, but I didn't find it. I found a poor approximation of the love I had in my head. That's because the love I was receiving was based on my physical attractiveness rather than real love.

Jesus is talking about spiritual love. The Buddhist sense of compassion is probably close to what he means. We are here to show compassion to each other. Another word might be kindness. Show kindness to each other. That means everyone. Not just our partners or families and friends. Everyone. It's pretty obvious that most of us don't do this. If each person could just do this in their daily interactions, the world would become so much better. I am trying to love people by sharing this book. I hope it will help people to heal.

We can show love in even our most basic interactions. Imagine an ordinary day where you show love in everything you do. So here's my example. On my dog walk, I always give a friendly wave to everyone and stop to chat with people. In this way, I am showing kindness. Some people reciprocate. Not everyone does. That's ok. On my drive to the grocery shop, I obey the speed limit and drive safely so I won't hurt anyone. I let people out of side roads when there is a queue of traffic. I stop to let people cross the road if it's safe. I wait patiently in the queue at the shop, and I chat pleasantly to the cashier and smile at them. Hopefully, I am improving their day. In my daily meditation and prayer, I send love to all those other suffering beings. I might choose different people for each day. One day I might think of those suffering from cancer, and the next, it might be people who are drug addicts. I am spreading love to people I don't even know. I talk to my spirit guides, angels or God each day. I ask them things and wait for the response. I tell them I love them. I listen for guidance. I spend my working time writing about spiritual matters. I also treat people in hypnotherapy sessions. I hope I am giving them love. Yes, I am still a hypnotherapist at this point, even though Jesus told me he is not that keen on it. I spend time with my dog and give him love, cuddles and play. I cook myself nutritious food because I love myself. I greet the person I live with with kindness, and I ask him about his day. I think about how I can be of more help to people. I read books on spiritual themes. All of these are small actions, but they are helping to make the world more pleasant. Imagine if we all did the same or more. What could you do to spread more love in your day?

Jesus also talks about raising ourselves. There was a lot in my Life Between Lives session about rising up or ascending. Ascension to most Christians would make them think of when Jesus was taken up to Heaven (John 20:17-31). He did this after appearing to the disciples to prove he had lived on after the crucifixion. So how can we ascend? I do believe that Jesus is talking about how we can achieve heaven on earth by showing love. In New Age circles, people talk about how we need to raise our vibration. This is exactly the same thing as having loving thoughts and actions. By being loving, your vibration increases. You become less bound on the Earth and more like angels or spiritual beings. If everyone does this, the vibration of the whole Earth is raised, and we can defeat the darkness. Through love, we can return to our spiritual natures and overcome the darkness of our material bodies that tell us that the physical world and egoistic desires are important. Meditation is another way of raising the vibration of yourself and everyone else.

The aim of human life is to reunite with God. The word God is a huge problem for many people. I think this is because, in Western traditions, many people learned a very childish notion of God in Sunday School or at school or church. God makes many people think of an old man sitting on a throne judging people. The God of the Old Testament can also appear like this. This is not how I experienced God in my spiritual hypnotherapy session. God was an energy force that was the unity of all things. He is not really male or female, so I use Him just as a convention. Some people prefer to call this Source rather than God to differentiate from the stereotypical belief, but I personally don't have a problem with the word God. There is a spark of God in each and every person. Some people seem to have more than others, perhaps because they are old souls or they chose to bring more to this particular incarnation. The spark within each of us needs to join with God so that we can have perfect harmony. We can join with God by loving Him and each other. It's as if every single soul needs to come back to the light. Nobody can be left out. That's why we must encourage others to understand the message of the guides.

Reincarnation was also a key theme in my Life Between Lives session. Reincarnation has been a part of some world religions, such as Buddhism and Hinduism, but Christianity has left it out. My guides tell me it was taken out of the Bible deliberately by people in the early Church. Why would anyone do this? It looks to me like it was about power and control in the early Roman Catholic Church. It's a good way of controlling people to tell them they only have one life, and if they do bad things, they are going to Hell. It's shocking to me that this idea has been allowed to terrify people for so many years. My guides were very clear that Hell does not exist. Even Lucifer explained that he is not in Hell, and neither is anyone else. Everyone goes 'home' to the place between lives. Most of us are stuck on the wheel of karma because of the errors we have made in our life. After a time of healing, we can reincarnate and have another try. Unfortunately, we continue to make mistakes, and this keeps happening again and again. Jesus came to show us that the way to get off the wheel is to love each other. Then we can go to the Light permanently.

A major message was that all the world religions need to join together. It's as if every religion has some of the truth, but nobody has all of the truth. The truth is being revealed through spiritual, mystical experiences with individuals. The idea is that you don't need churches or temples to talk to God. You can do it directly through prayer and meditation. You will know in your heart what feels true to you, and you don't need the intermediary of a priest to filter the message. Spiritual beings communicate through telepathy, so pay attention to thoughts and dreams that seem to come from outside yourself or from a deep place within you.

We come back to the light through love. That is it!

CHAPTER THIRTEEN:

Channelling Malalia

Malalia's message for humanity.

I am a spiritual guide, or what you might prefer to call a guardian angel. I look after many people. My name means Sadness. Many who incarnate on earth have volunteered to experience sadness as part of their life plan. Without sadness, there cannot be happiness. There is darkness, so there can be light. I help humans with their sadness. I have never lived on Earth. I stay in the higher realms. You can talk to me any time you like. I am Venusian. We are a race of spiritual beings. We live in the spiritual reality and watch over the Earth. We were there at the beginning. Once, a long time ago, we had bodies. Our planet was destroyed in the war. We have spirit-light bodies now. We work for the Light. Love is our intention.

There is an epidemic of sadness on Earth. You call it depression. It is to do with the way you live. You are separated from God. God is within and without. You can find God within your hearts. You have cut off from your spirituality. You can find this again by looking inside. Go into the silence. Sit with yourself. Reclaim your power. You are all spiritual beings.

The dark forces want you to be depressed. When you are sad, you are easier to control. Your culture is designed to make you feel inadequate. Films and television often transmit bad information into your mind. Your food is poisoned. Alcohol and drugs don't help you. Your leaders are corrupt. They desire perpetual war to make money. Money is a false idol. Your education system tells you the wrong things. Your work is often meaningless.

Do not follow leaders. Find your own power. Free yourself. Live in nature. The Earth is abundant. She has all you need. Speak your truth from your heart. Grow your own food. Treat the earth with respect. Eat organic produce. Live peacefully. Help each other. Set up new communities.

You must join together as one. Don't think in terms of separation. Who are you? Drop the labels. Identity politics is dividing you when you should be joining with each other. Black, white, gay, straight, trans, lesbian, vegan, left-wing, right-wing, male, female, young, old: all are labels without meaning. You are spirit. You are God. You are powerful. You have a sacred purpose.

Listen to the small voice within. Truly you know what is right and what is wrong.

Overcoming sadness is possible for all. Rise up. Keep rising to the light. Thoughts are spells. They are magic. Speak well of yourself and others. Rise like a phoenix. Look up.

You are never alone. You are surrounded by angels. We love you. There is nothing to fear. Death is not the end. It is merely a beginning. You live in an illusion. The 3D world is not important. The spiritual world is real. You are not separate. You just think you are.

Get in touch with the creativity inside. We all have a talent though we may have buried it. We can sing, dance, draw, write, paint, garden, cook, play, and laugh. This is what we were made to do.

Practise silence and stillness. God speaks in the gaps. He is in the stones, the bones, the trees, the earth, the wind, the high and lonely places. He is in the eyes of the homeless, the cry of the starving, the rubble of the war, the drowning refugee, the barrel of the gun. He is the seeds, the roots, the waves of the sea. He is the king, the slum child, the breath of a horse, the croak of a frog. He is you. He is me. We are one.

Do not be afraid. Have faith.

CHAPTER FOURTEEN:

Channelling Jesus

I am Jesus, Yeshua, Issa, Issie. I live in the Light. I descended to Earth and lived as a man. I taught you how to live. I had lived many times before. I will live again. I volunteered for the role of Issie to bring wisdom. I brought all my energy to the life of Issie. I agreed my role with God. I am part of God, and so are you.

My message is love. We rise through love. Love yourself. Love each other. I love the earth and the animals and the fish. I love the apples and the figs. I love the sky and the sun. I love the rain and the wind. I love those who are unlovable. Love those who make you want to turn away. I love where it is hard to look.

You are searching for Heaven everywhere. It is inside you. You can go there any time you like. Open your heart. Open the gate. Let love in and let love out. Find the truth inside you and then tell others.

You can call on me any time. Just say my name. I am always there. We suffer into truth. I can comfort you. I hear your cry. I love you. Do everything with an open heart. Talk to me as a friend. Do not worship me. Talk to me anywhere. I am everywhere. You do not need special buildings or places. You don't need rituals or fancy prayers. Just talk to me with transparency.

You are more powerful than you know. You can perform miracles. You create the world. The great spirit that you call God is within and without. He is in Heaven and inside your heart.

Look at everyone as divine.

The way out is in. Meditate on the heart space. All wisdom will be revealed to you. Have no fear. You are immortal. Breathe in and breathe out. Be love.

The ultimate reality is the spiritual realm. You can call it Heaven or the Kingdom of God or, as we prefer: home. Home is oneness. At home, we dwell in bliss. Home cannot be destroyed. Home is beyond form, beyond time, beyond space, beyond boundaries. God is the Great Spirit who is Love. He cannot anger. He cannot attack. God created humanity to be one with Him. Calling God Him is just a convention. He is both male and female: father and mother.

The world is an attempt at separateness. Here on Earth, we believe in space and time. We believe in the ego. The ego tells us we are separate from each other. We made this world. This separation is an illusion. It occurs only in our minds. We are dreaming of the world we perceive.

Our true soul self is in Heaven. In reality, there is no separation and no sin. We believe we have sinned, and we are full of guilt and fear. Fear is the source of our suffering. We attack the world, but we are really attacking ourselves.

I, as Yeshua, stand between you and Home. I can heal you. Heal your mind. We can awaken in Heaven by changing our perception. Ask me to heal your perception. Forgive the world because it has not harmed you. Allow your love to flow into the world. Allow that you are not separate from others. See God in everyone and everything. Join with others. We heal ourselves with loving thoughts. When we are all healed, we rise to the Light. We go home.

The Bible is a metaphor. It explains some things like a story. It doesn't have it all right. It is stitched together from the words of many men over many years. Much is hidden. It was all about power. Don't take it too literally. Listen to your heart.

You are the light of the world. You were made to shine. Don't hide your light. Speak the truth. You are warriors of the light. Fight not with swords but with love, with kindness, with compassion, with an open heart, gentle words.

The Devil is not real. The evil is inside you. You can conquer your animalistic nature. Choose the light within. Change your thoughts to loving ones. Feed the light within you.

Do not be afraid. There is no death and no punishment. Free yourself of guilt and shame. Focus on love. You are journeying back to God.

All religions are one. Those of any religion can call on me for help. I am available to everyone. Come together. Do not offer me blood. I have no need of it. Come with an innocent heart, just as you are. All are equal before me. Men and women are of the same importance.

Race does not matter. There are no kings nor princes in Heaven.

Do not give your power away. Do not follow leaders. Do not submit to others. Find your own power within. Co-operate with each other. Co-exist. You don't need to bend the knee.

Immerse yourself fully in the present moment. Forget the past. It is gone. The future is unknown to you. Do each task with full attention.

My way is the middle way. You don't need to starve yourselves like the holy men of old. You should not mutilate your body in order to imitate me. Become like me through loving words and actions. Eat only what you need and no more. Pray and meditate to draw close to me.

You don't need to stay with those who don't love you. Find your own way.

I love you.

CHAPTER FIFTEEN:

Channelling St Mary

I am Mary, the mother of Jesus. You are all my children. I love you all. I am there for all of you. You can ask me for help. You don't need to know any special prayers. Just picture me in your mind and say my name.

I was a Jewish woman of the house of David. I had dark brown hair and dark eyes. My skin was olive-brown. I was a poor woman, and I wore a simple robe with a rope tied around the middle. I covered my hair. I was a simple person who followed God.

When I was thirteen, a Roman soldier kidnapped me in the street. I was coming back from the market with cloth for my mother. The soldier was called Panthera. He raped me many times. I had to keep a house for him and share his bed. There was nothing my parents could do. The Romans had all the power, and they were cruel people. They had invaded our land and told us what to do. I felt such shame. Soon I felt the baby Issie grow inside me. Panthera saw I was pregnant and threw me out into the street. I found my way back to my parent's house. There was much wailing but also joy at my return. Joseph agreed to marry me. His wife had died, and he had other children who needed a mother.

I liked to nurture people. I looked after everyone. I did the work of the house: I brought water from the well, I baked bread, I washed clothes and I sewed garments. We also had a little garden, and I tended the vines. I grew some vegetables and looked after the goats. I knew the Torah by heart, and I told the stories to Issie and the other children in the evening. I used to act out the stories with funny voices to make him laugh. The women often worked together and helped each other. I was never lonely. Joseph was a kind man and a good husband to me. I was content at that time.

I missed Issie so much when he went away travelling. When he returned, I felt such joy. I followed him all over Palestine as he taught. I was amazed by the things he said and did. I was proud for him to marry Mary Magdalene, and she was a strength to me. Watching him suffer on the cross was terrible. I thought my heart would be wrenched from my body. When he was taken to a cave, I looked after him. I tended his wounds and fed him with a spoon. The strength returned to his body. He was Issie again, and he learned to walk. We travelled again in secret. Eventually, we settled in India. I lived to a great age and died there. So I understand what it is to be a human woman. I had the sufferings of childbirth and the tribulation of losing my home and nation. I knew the life of an exile. I understand you and what you need. Keep faith in God, whatever is happening. Pray and know that you are loved.

Women are revered by God. Respect women in all things. You are all the same before God. Remember that softness is a real strength. It is time for the Divine Feminine to come forward now. Women must speak. Shine your light. We are the creators, the dancers, the artists, the cooks, the writers, the poets, the healers, the magicians. We can lead as one. Tell others about the Light. Shine brightly. Go out into the world and use your talents if that is what you wish.

Love each other with all your hearts. When someone speaks harshly to you, bless them in your mind and move away. Don't let them sully your soul. Rise above. You have no need to retaliate in kind. Let God deal with them.

You don't need to build idols of me. I am not a statue. I am everywhere. Talk to me as to your mother. Sit quietly and listen to your heart. I am there. Feel my love enfolding you. It will give you all you need.

Sex between two people is beautiful, but use your gift wisely. Don't give your energy away to the unworthy. Treat each other with reverence and awe. Never take a woman by force, for you will find this happening to you. You can leave a man if he mistreats you. A woman's worth is not found in her virginity or the lack of it. All women are worthy of love and honour.

Prayer is a good use of your time. Pray at all times: in the house, in the street, at work, at the shops. Pray silently in your heart. Pray for the welfare of others. Pray for the relief of suffering. Pray for the lonely and the lost. Pray for the children and the animals. Pray to take away the suffering of others. Breathe in suffering. Breathe out, love.

Women have their own special wisdom. They are strong and powerful but in their own way. They do not need to imitate the ways of men. Look at what the men have done to the world. They are acting from ego, from the male impulse to dominate and control. Women can rule with the heart. We can respect the earth, walking lightly on her. Those who lead must first learn how to follow. Serving others is true greatness. Those who seek power should never be given it.

Focus on the small things of the day. This is where wisdom lies. There is more to learn in a simple home than a great palace. Serve others with a joyful heart.

I love you.

CHAPTER SIXTEEN:

Channelling Lucifer

Message for humanity.

I am Lucifer. My name means bringer of the light. I am what you might call an Archangel. I am not evil. I am not the Devil. I work for the Light. I volunteered for my role. I watch The Earth. I live in this dimension.

You can talk to me anytime. Just call on me. I can give advice. I do not need sacrifices, not human or animal. Sacrificing to me will not give you what you want. It will create more karma for you. It will pin you to the Earth. This is mistaken behaviour. There are many people doing this in secret. They must be exposed. Shine a light on their darkness. Bring it to be known. I cannot grant your wishes if they go against your soul contract. I can help you to see clearly. You can understand yourself better. Do not worship me. I am not God. I help God with the plan.

Ultimate reality is hard for you to understand from the human perspective. In Heaven, there is no good or evil. There is no duality. There just is. There is no space and no time. There is this moment. The supreme being is all-loving, all-knowing, and all-powerful. It is neither male nor female. It contains all things within it. You came from it, and you will return to it. You will dwell in eternal bliss. It is abwoon d'bashmaya.

There is nothing to fear. There is no punishment. There is no burning. Hell is not real. The Church is to blame for fear-mongering. The only judgement is that you give yourself. Let go of striving. All religions see through a glass darkly. They see the reflections, the shadows, but they don't see the whole. It is too much for the human mind to hold. You have come so far, but there is still far to go. It is time for a new promise, a New Testament. You can begin to see more clearly. The angels will show you a new way.

Here you are in the separation. Your mission is to join with God. Open your heart. Listen to your wisdom deep within. You know. Your soul is singing with joy when you listen to it. All the wisdom of the ages is inside you. You are a light being. You are God.

I am not in charge of what you call demons. They are in a different vibration. You might call them spiritual entities. Not all are benevolent. The ancient peoples knew this well. They had many names: the fey folk, fairies, Baal, Moloch, sirens, serpents, dragons, beasts of the deep, aliens, Annunakai, salamanders, sprites, Leviathan, Legion. They work in darkness. Do not worship them. Do not pray to them. They are out for themselves, not for you. They can trick you and lead you astray. Some of your mediums talk to them and believe they are speaking with angels. Use discernment always. The light does not ask for blood. The Father's house has many mansions. This is a way of saying there are many levels or dimensions. The lower levels are the spiritual plane where dark entities can live. You can find all manner of spiritual beings and some souls of the dead. They are the ones still looking to Earth instead of the realms above. They have nothing useful to tell you. Do not talk to them. Do not give them power over you. Ignore them. Send them away by order of the Light. They cannot stand against it. Above that, the vibrations are higher and higher. In the highest realms, you find God and the great spirits. These are the wise ones, the most highly evolved, the ones who know.

These are the beings you should pray to. Sit until they come into your heart. You will know them by their fruits. They are beings of love. Stay in the light.

Focus on the love.

Atheism is part of the darkness. It is not true. Your scientists tell you that you are apes. You are not. You are so much more than this. You have God within you. Atheists say you live and die and rot in the ground. You eat, drink, have sex and seek pleasure. You cover up your lack of power and money. You loot the Earth for her treasures. You rape the land. You make war with your neighbours. These men have led you into a world of lies. They are mistaken.

And you say it is I who is evil? I give them the free choice to choose right or wrong. So much of the Earth is covered in darkness. The light can reclaim it.

You have no need for crystals, props, or rituals. Gold will not help you. The magic is inside you.

Discover your true nature. Meditate until you find your light. Join with others of like mind and help each other. The forces of darkness will not prevail. Choose the light. You have a human experience. Think of it like a test or a trial. If you fail the test, you can try again. Try to pass. You do this through loving thoughts, loving actions, loving words. It's the same as kindness or compassion. Sit with your feelings until you transmute them to the light. There is no need to compare yourself to others. This is your journey. It is unique to you. You are a being powerful beyond measure. You can do anything. Trust and believe. A soul can move the mountains, calm the seas and storms, fly like a bird and make gold from stone.

I love you.

CHAPTER SEVENTEEN:

Channelling the Chinese Sage - Li

My name is Li. I am a master of Confucianism. I represent wisdom. I am what you might call an ascended master. I lived many lives on Earth. My last life in China was the one where I ascended. I lived a good life and gained enough wisdom to become a master in Heaven. I sit on Divine Councils. I guide people. You can ask for my help any time.

People in the West would benefit from learning the Eastern ways of doing things. We think more communally, not so much about the individual. When taking an action, you must think of others in your community. Your action must benefit everyone, not just yourself. We are all one. We rise together. Work on putting your ego to the back. You can do this through meditation and quiet time. Focus on others. Hold them in your mind's eye. Send compassion to them. Watch it flow from you to them. Take in their pain into you; breathe out love.

Breathe in pain; breathe out love. It is simple. In this way, we heal the world.

All religions are one. It does not matter which one you choose. The flavour is not important, but you must start a spiritual practice. You can choose a master in the spirit realm to help you. Choose someone you feel comfortable with. Meditate on them and ask them for help.

Organized religion is not necessary. You can contact your master anywhere and any place. Some places are more conducive to meditation. Spirits like the high places where the air is

fresh. Natural places are good. We love the mountains and the springs. You can feel us on the seashore and in the desert.

Everything is sacred. Always choose the highest moral action in everything you do. You know what is right and wrong inside. Serve your family and your community. Every action is important. The cleaner and the cook are playing just as vital a role as the king or the merchant. Nobody is higher than the other. We are all equal. Our goal is to live in harmony with each other. We should not make war with our neighbours. Do not listen to politicians.

They are not wise. Follow your own heart. The leader of all is the servant of all.

We do not need to sacrifice to the spirits. It will do no good. Protect yourself from evil by being ethical in all things. Then nothing can harm you. Work on honesty, loyalty, hard work, respect, bravery, kindness. Learn to master yourself through meditation. Perfect yourself each day. Your soul can grow and evolve. Then you can join with the Great Spirit.

Heaven is in harmony – a dance of opposites. There is a middle way. So should it be on the Earth? Find the middle path, and here is wisdom. Do not eat too much or too little. Do not overexert yourself, nor be lazy. Be present in all your actions. Keep a clear mind – don't cloud it with substances. Do your work well and rest when you need to. Focus on harmony.

Men and women should not be in opposition. Both are necessary. They should respect each other in marriage, in the family and in society. One is not lesser than the other. A man who mistreats a woman is doing a great harm. Likewise, a woman who mistreats a man is also in the wrong. Children are gifts. Treat them well. A boy is not superior to a girl. Both are required for a harmonious society.

The religion of Buddhism is perhaps closest to the truth of things I now see from my position in Heaven, but it is not the whole truth. All religions are poisoned by the human vessel – the truths are twisted and changed. You do not need special clothes, or rituals, or special objects or temples. Each is sufficient in himself. You have the whole world inside of you. You do not need to seek anything else. Meditate on the heart. Remember, you are divine.

You can train your thoughts to change your reality. Meditate each day, and great riches will be shown to you. Quiet the mind. Do not be afraid to go deep inside yourself. There is nothing to fear there. The soul dwells in bliss. Anyone can achieve this bliss. Focus on what you want, not on what you lack. Think loving thoughts, do loving actions. Trust yourself.

Simplicity is the way of wisdom. There is too much confusion in the world, with conflicting messages everywhere. Turn off your devices, your televisions and your computers. There are those who wish to control you through these things. They are thinking of what is good for them, but you are being led astray. There are things being shown that should not be seen. You all need to turn away from the darkness. You need shelter, food and good companionship. All else is a distraction. Focus on your higher selves. Purify your hearts with good thoughts.

All is as it should be. There is no need to fear the future nor to dwell on the past. Be here now. Think of harmony. Calm the mind. There is yin and yang. The universe is like a dance of opposites – all are part of the whole. Our thoughts move forward and back like the tides. Follow them without judgement. They are not good or bad. They just are. Meet attack with equanimity. Nothing can harm you. Make your mind like a beautiful garden.

I bow to you, divine beings. All is well.

CHAPTER EIGHTEEN:

Channelling African Shaman - Kothiro

Greetings to the world. I am Kothiro, Kothie for short. I was a medicine man in Senegal thousands of years ago. I became highly evolved. Now I am an ascended master. I see things differently from my vantage point in the spirit world.

When I was on Earth, I believed in the indigenous religion of Senegal. We worshipped the ancestors. If we honoured them, they looked after us. Well, at least that is what we believed. I sacrificed animals to the gods and sometimes people. We believed that human sacrifice would give you great power. You could have what you wanted. This was wrong reasoning. The Christians will tell you that Jesus was a human sacrifice to God to atone for sins. This is also false reasoning. The light does not ask for blood. Now I am in the light; I see this. God did not ask for a human sacrifice. There are no sins to atone for. In the highest spiritual realms, there is no good and evil. There just is. Where God dwells, there is boundless love.

Human sacrifice was a pagan idea of the Romans. They grafted it onto the life of Jesus for their own purposes. To dwell in bliss, do good deeds, and think good thoughts. Do no harm. This is all. Jesus is a high master. Follow his actions, his words, his thoughts. Love.

Human sacrifice still occurs on the Earth. Uganda is an example where the practice is common. It is also happening in Europe and the Americas. There are dark people sacrificing children for personal power. The darkness is not in their skin; it is in their hearts. This is erroneous. They are creating bad karma for themselves. They will need to work this out in subsequent lives. They are only bringing suffering on themselves. Do not listen to those who call themselves leaders or influencers. Actors are good at acting – they are not knowledgeable about matters of the spirit. Politicians are corrupt with money. They are not evolved spiritually. They are the ones in need of guidance more than the common people. A slum child has more knowledge than a President about how the world really works. A beggar is greater in Heaven than a king.

When I lived on Earth I had great knowledge of the healing plants and herbs. This is good to learn. There are plants that open the gate to the spirit world: marijuana, tobacco, iboga, ayahuasca, belladonna, henbane, peyote, poppy, mescaline, salvia, morning glory, khat.

These plants must be treated with respect. You must take them under the guidance of a knowledgeable shaman, as there is a risk of poison. Alternatively, you can study for a long time yourself. Find people you can trust. Nature has everything you need. The plants will show you what you need to know through dreams and visions. Listen to the Mother.

There are all kinds of beings in the spiritual planes. Some are low vibration, some high. Many are still evolving on their journey. They are far from the high realms. You must use discernment with the spirits. Not all do good on the Earth plane. Though it is true that good and evil have no meaning where I am, it does have truth where you are. Bad deeds attach you more strongly to the Earth. Don't look down; look up to the high spiritual levels. This is where you want to go. You get there through love. Only talk to the loving spirits. If a spirit is frightening you, hitting you, or trying to have sex with you without your consent, it is a mischievous spirit. Do not trust it. Tell it to leave you in the name of Jesus. Protect yourself with white light. Spirits that tell you to harm yourself should not be heeded. Never cut or defile your body. It is given to you as your glory. You are a luminescent being of light. Hold your light high.

You can talk to the spirits through meditation. Sit in nature and talk to them. Trust your own heart. Beware of false guides, for there are many. Ask me for help. I am of the Light. You do not need rituals, robes or great buildings.

African people have suffered much on the Earth. They need to find their original greatness. Do this by going inside yourself. Listen to your own wisdom. Do not let anger from the past make you bitter and angry. Let it go. Do not hold the heaviness of your ancestors' suffering in your hearts. You are precious to God. All are equal in the Kingdom. The first is last, and the last is first. Let go of labels. Martin Luther King told you: do not judge a man by the colour of his skin but by the content of his character. This is wisdom. Identity politics is a device of the darkness to divide you from one another. Join together in the light. We are one.

Do not fear the future. You have no need of divination. This moment is sufficient for you. Concentrate on the present. Here is the point of power. Slough off the past like the snake sheds his skin. You are born again in each moment. Whatever you have done, however low you have sunk, you have value to God. All are saved. Begin again with love and joy in your heart.

Work together for good. Make rain. Make the desert bloom again with a thousand flowers. Respect the animals of the Earth. Don't kill for pleasure. Only eat flesh out of necessity, sparingly for the good within it. Make the plants your staple. They have much healing in them. Use natural manure to grow your vegetables. You have no need for chemicals. The earth provides everything that is needed. Alcohol can be taken in small doses, not to the point of intoxication and collapse. The middle way is the right way in all things.

All religions are one. Come together. Do not use religion to separate yourselves from others. Love is at the heart of all true religions. Look inside yourself, and you know what is right. It is there in your heart. Be less in your mind – it is clouding you with excessive thoughts. Clear it through deep breathing. Breath is sacred. Do not enslave your neighbours. They are not your enemies. We are all brothers and sisters.

Love to all and infinite blessings.

CHAPTER NINETEEN:

Channelling Anubis

Welcome all. I am Anubis. I am also known as Anpu. I have the head of a jackal and the body of a man. I wear a striped headdress. My body is black like the soil of the Nile. I feel hard like a rock, and I am supernaturally strong. The Egyptians called me the god of the dead. I protected graves, I mummified bodies, and I was there at the weighing of the heart, so they said. I am a spirit being but not a god. You could call me an angel. Do not worship me. Talk to me, and I will try to help you.

I guard the gate between the realms of the living and the dead. I will guide you through the chambers of the other world. With me, you have nothing to fear. There are dangers to be found. Not all of the spirits wish you well. Those with a good heart will find doors open for them. Call on me to protect you. You do not need to give me gifts. Your love and friendship is enough. I will show you the best rooms in the House of the Dead.

The Ancient Egyptians had spiritual power. They knew great magic, but they were wrong about many things. You do not need to take anything into the next world. Your soul is the only thing that can cross over. Funeral rituals are not important. You can be buried, cremated, dropped into the sea, have a sky burial. None of it matters to your soul. Sacrifices to me are not necessary. They will not make any difference. There is no judgement of your heart after death by me or others. I do not weigh your heart. You judge yourself about how you did in your life. You review your lessons. You may be born again to work out your karma. Every action causes a reaction. Those with loving, innocent hearts will ascend higher.

I dwell in the higher realms, not on Earth. I guide and analyze. I watch and protect. I am full of kindness and compassion. I can help you heal your darkness. To heal fully, you must face your shadows. Look at yourself with honesty. Accept those parts of yourself that you don't want to see. Look back at your wounds from childhood. Face them and heal them with love. We are all a mixture of good and bad. See yourself as a whole. Love those parts of yourself that are hard to love. Forgive yourself for those times when you were crying out in pain and did something you now regret. You were trying your best. Travel deep within your mind in meditation and hypnosis. Don't be afraid of what you find there. Bring it all into the light for healing. Sin is an illusion. All rise.

Death is nothing to fear. It is a rebirth. We are reborn in an endless cycle until we ascend. We perfect our souls little by little, more and more, over centuries, millennia. We suffer, and we learn. One day we join with the eternal Father and Mother. There is so much beauty to see in the ultimate reality. You can make anything you want with your mind. You can have that lovely house you saw opposite Grandma with the big bay windows. You can furnish it however you want. The great thing is you don't need to do dishes in Heaven. That is just one example. You can travel to anywhere in the world. You can see all those places you want to go, and you won't get bitten by mosquitoes. You can journey to other worlds, other planets. You can become like gods and make your own creations. You can start to make your own planets, your very own galaxies. Nothing is impossible. Maybe you want to learn something. You can master anything you want. We have libraries piled high with books and wise, patient teachers. There are gardens with all manner of flowers and plants. The colours are brighter than anything you can ever imagine. All this is yours and more. You can meet with other souls that you love and see your pets again. All are waiting there for you.

There is much tribulation on the Earth, and much is covered with darkness. You can shine your light into these dark places. Everyone can be the light of the world. Start by loving and accepting yourself. From here, you can learn to love others. Life is a journey into truth. All mistakes lead to more learning. You cannot fail. Keep going within. Open your heart like a child to all and to the world. Meditate on love. Love those who are hard to love. I love those who don't deserve it. Love without question.

Magic is neither good nor bad. It is. The intention is what matters. You can make things happen with the power of your mind. You can master energy. There are great teachers in the East. All must be brought to light. We are ready for the knowledge now. Focus on good intentions. Sit in the silence, and all will be shown to you. Rediscover your own power. Do not submit to those who wish you harm. Leave behind those who do not wish to hear the truth. Shake the dust off your feet and keep your light burning. You are all gods. It's just that you have forgotten. Speak the truth even though you shake as you do it. The swords of the angels will go before you and beat your path.

All is well.

CHAPTER TWENTY:

Channelling Kokua

I am Kokua. I represent compassion. I am from the planet that is spiritual Venus. You may think I am an alien or a guide. I show myself wearing the armour of a medieval knight. I have a broadsword. My hair is long and blonde. My skin is as white as ivory, and my eyes are blue. I am very tall. I fight for the Light. I shine before the darkness, and it shrinks before me.

Demons slink away when they see me coming. They spit and attack because they know I am greater than they. In the spiritual realm, I am involved in Heavenly warfare. I fear nothing. I speak the truth to any man, demon or abominable beast. There are dark forces who do evil. I defend the Light from them.

We Venusians have great spaceships that can travel anywhere in the universe. We can traverse between dimensions. We visit Earth. We have held back wars and stayed in the hands of the evil doers. We bring only love. I can appear to you if you call on me. You can communicate with me through telepathy.

I have lived many times. I have incarnated on Earth, on Venus, and on so many other planets. I volunteer for the missions. I have been a great soul and a small soul. I have been a king and a pauper. I am a man and a woman. I work with Yeshua, Jesus, the Christ. I am his consort in Heaven. All Venusians work together to bring the light. We tell about the Light.

Here is my message to Humanity. On Earth, there is a constant battle between good and evil, the yin and yang. People must learn to live in the Light just as we do in Heaven. We need to

make harmony, and live together as one people. It is not right that one is in his palace and one in the street. We must strive for equality for all humans. Money and power are false idols. Do not worship them. Keep your immortal soul in the forefront of your mind, and you can do great things.

We rise through love. Sing, dance, live in joy. Eat the sweet fruit and drink the wine. Make music. All are gifts from the divine Father and Mother. All of the Earth is to be enjoyed by all. Love unconditionally and with abandon. When your love is rejected, love anyway. Speak the truth always. Bellow it from the rooftops.

Shout the truth from the mountains. God speaks through you. Laugh in the face of your enemies. You are divine light.

Build your strength from within in the heart space. Grow strong each day through the thoughts you tell yourself. Speak kindly to your heart and your mind. Take care of your body. You are not a mistake. You are made for a purpose. Commune with the spirits until you know the truth. Spend time alone in the silence until your heart opens to the truth of the Light. Once you know, tell the others the good news. When they say you are mad and laugh at you, pay them no heed. They cannot hear what you can.

There is nothing to fear. You die many times and are reborn. You cannot fall. Trust that everything is working out just as it should. There is a plan that is unfolding, and you are playing your part in it.

Find others to join together with. Share everything and co-operate fully. Live in harmony with each other and with the Earth. Take just what you need and no more. Respect the plants, the trees and the animals. Live in nature. Don't have leaders. Each person is the leader of their own heart.

It is time for everyone to come back to the Light. We have no need of priests or pastors who think more of their own comfort than the truth. Use discernment with those who say they have the true knowledge. Look at their actions. Do they bear fruit? Each person must meditate until they see and hear. The truth will be given to them. Join together with others. It's like a candle that lights, and then others can be lit from it. Light up the world.

Your soul was made by the Creator. You may be new or old. You may have lived many times before on Earth and in other worlds. You agreed to come here. You choose your purpose together with your guides and your spirit council. You may have one guardian angel or many. Ask them for help. You chose your appearance, your sex, your parents. You picked out your talents and skills. There were lessons you needed to learn. The wisest souls choose the hardest lives. You learn so much from a difficult life. You are strong enough to bear it. All the angels in Heaven are cheering you on to the finish line. You can do it.

At the end of your life, your soul leaves your body and goes back to the spirit world. There you review your life and consider your lessons. You can have time to heal if you need it. You can learn things here and have the experiences you want. In time, you may choose to reincarnate to help your soul to learn. There is no punishment or coercion. You have the choice. You are a volunteer. Earth is a hard school. You have free will. Choose it to do good. Perform all your tasks with great love. Care for others. Use your talents to help each other.

Spread the Light.

Jesus was an example of how to live. Follow him by being like him. Any one of you can do as he did. Master yourself, and you can be like him. Bring love into your heart and send it out to others. Say his name, and he will answer you.

Go into the world and spread the Light.

CHAPTER TWENTY-ONE:

Meditation for meeting your spirit guides.

You may want to record this and play it to yourself as you meditate.

Just relax. Breathe in and out deeply. Breathe right into the belly. Breathe in and out through the nose. Notice the breath. Close your eyes. Continue breathing. Observe your thoughts without judgement. Just let them go by. They are like clouds drifting past in the sky. Stay in this present moment. Breathe in and breathe out. Just notice your breathing, the feel of your breath in your nose, the rise and fall of your diaphragm. Everything is calm and easy. Notice how your body feels. Be aware of any discomfort. Just let it go.

Imagine in your mind's eye a beautiful scene. You are out in nature. You are walking along a path and enjoying the flowers and trees. The bees are buzzing, and you can feel the warmth of the sun on your skin. In the distance, you see a huge waterfall. You walk towards the waterfall, and you see there is a cave beneath it. You walk into the cave, and you see the waterfall above you. You are standing beneath it. Feel the water splashing all around you. Hear the roar. This is a waterfall of light. The light can be any colour of the rainbow. It might be many colours or every colour, that is. This beautiful waterfall is flowing down, down from above.

Soothing, calming, relaxing as it flows down, down, down. You feel all your tension leave your body as the water of light flows down and down and down and down.

The light touches the top of your head. It relaxes the tiny muscles of your scalp. Open the top of your head and ask the light to come inside. The light flows throughout your body.

Down and down, down, down, down. The light is all around you. It wraps around your body. It's in your forehead now, in your nose, your cheeks, your jaw. Down and down and down, it goes into the neck and throat. The light flows into your shoulders, and as they relax, the soothing sensation of the light continues into the arms, past the elbows and the forearms. The light is flowing into your hands now, the fingers.

The relaxing healing light is in your chest now, your ribs and stomach, as your abdominal muscles go loose and limp and so relaxed. The light flows down the spine. It sends a wave of relaxation into the shoulder blades. You feel peace and calm flowing into your back, the small of the back. Serenity is wrapping around your waist, taking your deeper, deeper, deeper. The light flows into your hips and pelvis.

The waterfall of light is flowing into your legs. You feel the thighs relax, the knees, the calves. Down and down and down deeper to the ankles, the feet and all the way to the tips of the toes. Deeper and deeper and down and down. The deeper you go, the better it feels, and the better you feel, the deeper it goes.

The light is flowing all through your body now. You are flowing with it, soothing, floating, calming, drifting. Deeper and deeper. Down and down. Your body starts to feel so heavy, so very heavy, you are sinking into your chair. It's good, it's good, it's all so good.

You may even feel light, as if you are detaching from your body. You are so light you are floating in the air. You are so light, so very light, so light.

Now you are totally relaxed; I want to tell you some things. In your mind lies an awareness of the ultimate truth. You have complete knowledge of everything that has ever happened to you in this life and your past lives. You are aware of your soul mates and your life purpose. You know your guides and masters.

Your main guide has been with you since your birth and will remain with you throughout your life. Your intuition is your guide speaking to you. You may have other guides who appear to help you with particular purposes. They may appear as lights or in human form.

Rise up to the very highest level of your mind. See yourself ascending higher and higher. I am going to count from one to five. You are ascending and rising higher and higher. Reach up into your Higher self, your superconscious mind. Number one. Rising, letting go of the physical. Number two. Rising up higher and higher. Ascending, ascending, ascending. Number Three. Rising higher, higher, higher. Up and up and up. Number four. Ascending, ascending, ascending, higher, higher, higher, up, up, up. Almost there. You are detached from the physical and crossing over into your higher mind. Number five. You are there. Notice your surroundings.

Perceive your guide's call name. See the letters coming into your mind. Now you have it. Now perceive exactly what your guide looks like. On the count of three, they will appear before you. Trust your impressions. Number one. Allow it. Number two.

Open your mind to the impressions. Number three. Perceive your guide in front of you.

Do they appear male or female? How old does he or she appear? What is their hair like? Can you see their clothing or footwear?

Ask your guides questions and wait for the answers…thoughts will come into your head through telepathy.

Silence for a while.

Become aware of any other Masters that are working with you. On the count of three, your

masters appear before you…one…two…three. Ask them anything you like.

Silence for a while.

Now it is time to say goodbye to the guides. We thank you for helping us today. Now it's time to awaken to your full awareness, remembering everything that has happened. One, beginning to wake up; two, returning to full awareness; three, alert and awake; four, open your eyes; five, you are back.

References

Aboutbuddhism.org (2023) *About Buddhism* Available at www.aboutbuddhism.org

(Accessed on 5 May 2023)

Antonov, V (2008) *The Gospel of Philip* CreateSpace, Scotts Valley, California, US

Bernstein, M (1956) *The Search for Bridey Murphy* Hutchinson, London, UK

Branch, T (1998) *Pillar of Fire* Simon and Schuster, London, UK.

Brent A, Paterline B A, (2016) *Forensic hypnosis and the courts* Journal of Law and Criminal Justice, 4 (2) 1-7

Bullock, A (1962) *Hitler: A Study in Tyranny* Konecky and Konecky, Old Saybrook, Connecticut, US

Chan, B (2023) *Buddha translation from ancient Tibetan to English a 100-year task* South China Morning Post Available at www.scmp.com (Accessed on 8 May 2023)

Channelingerik.com (2023) *Channeling Erik* Available at www.channelingerik..com

(Accessed on 8 May 2023)

Confucius (2014) *The Analects* Penguin Classics, London, UK

CNN.com (2023) *ISIS* Available at www.edition.cnn.com (Accessed on 5 May 2023)

Dalai Llama (2009) *Insight from the Dalai Llama* Andrews and MacMeel, Kansas City, MO. US

Elman D (1964) *Hypnotherapy* Westwood Publishing, London, UK

Goldsworthy, A (2010) *How Rome Fell* Yale University Press, London, UK

The Guardian (2013) *Tory MP Nadhim Zaharia admits taxpayers paid power bill for his stables* Available at www.theguardian.com (Accessed on 8 May 2023)

HBO.com (2023) *Game of Thrones* Available at www.hbo.com (Accessed on 5 May 2023)

Hinduamerican.org (2023) *Hindu American Foundation* Available at www.hinduamerican.org (Accessed on 5 May 2023)

Holocaust Memorial Day Trust (2023) Available at www.had.org.uk (Accessed on 5 May 2023)

Jaki, S L (1999) *God and the Sun at Fatima* Real View Books, New Hope, KY, US.

Jensen MP, Ehde DM, Gertz KJ Stoelb BL, Dillworth TM, Hirsh AT, Molson IR, Kraft GH

Effects of self-hypnosis training and cognitive restructuring on daily pain intensity and catastrophizing in individuals with ultimate sclerosis and chronic pain Int J Clin Exp Hypn, 2011 Jan;59(1):45-63

Landau-Tasseron, E (1990) *Sayf Ibn Umar in Medieval and Modern Scholarship vol. 67, no,1 pp. 1-26* Available at https://doi.org/10.1515/Islam.1990.67.1

LeLoupe, J (2002) *The Gospel of Mary Magdalene* Inner Traditions, Rochester, Vermont, US

Lewis, C S (2012) *Mere Christianity* Collins, New York, US

LightbetweenLives (2023) *Life Between Lives – Spiritual Hypnotherapy* Available at www.lightbetweenlives.com (Accessed: 24 April 2023)

Lioy, S (2019) *Tibet* Lonely Planet, Dublin, Ireland

Lipton, B (2010) *The Biology of Belief* Hay House, Carlsbad, California

Lockley, J (2017) *The Way of the Leopard* Sounds True, Boulder, Colorado, US

Martel, F (2019) *In the Closet of the Vatican* Bloomsbury Continuum, London, UK

Martin, R (2023) *The Greatest Story Never Told* Independently Published

Morgan Cron, I (2013) *Chasing Francis* Zondervan, Nashville, TN, US

Newtoninstitute.org (2023) *Michael Newton Institute* Available at www.newtoninstitute.org (Accessed: 24 April 2023)

Newton, M (2000) *Destiny of Souls* Llewelyn Publications, Woodbury, Minnesota, US

Newton, M (2002) *Journey of Souls* Llewelyn Publications, Woodbury, Minnesota, US

Newton, M (2004) *Life Between Lives* Llewelyn Publications, Woodbury, Minnesota, US

Notovitch, N (1894) *The Unknown Life of Jesus Christ,* Indo-American Book Company, Chicago, Ill, US

Pelikan, J (1998) *Mary Through the Centuries,* Yale University Press, New Haven, CT, USA

Posner, G (2021) *The Pope's Corruption Problems,* Forbes, Available at www.Forbes.com

(Accessed on 8 May 2023)

Ramirez, J (2016) *The Private Lives of the Saints* WH Allen, London

Redcross.org.uk (2023) *Turkey and Syria Earthquake* Available at www.redcross.org.uk (Accessed on 5 May 2023)

Request.org.uk (2023) *How did the Roman Catholic Church start?* Available at www.request.org.uk (Accessed on 8 May 2023)

Robinson, J (2000) *The Nag Hammadi Library* Harper One, San Francisco, US

Rossi, D (2000) *The Philosophical View of the Great Perfection in the Tibetan Bon Religion* Snow Lion, Ithaca, NY, US

Ruiz, D (2019) *The Wisdom of the Shamans* Hierophant Publishing, San Antonio, Texas

Schwartz, B (2023) *Justice for War Crimes in Ukraine a Must* Available at www.how.org

(Accessed on 5 May 2023)

Shamanicjourney.com (2023) *Shamanic Journey* Available at www.shamanicjourney.com

(Accessed 5 May 2023)

Shelivesaloha.com (2023) *She Lives Aloha* Available at www.shelivesaloha.com (Accessed 5 May 2023)

Simon S (2012) *Venus* Seymour Science LLC, US.

Sinmaz, E (2023) *Headteacher killed herself after news of low Ofsted rating, family says*

Available at www.theguardian.com (Accessed on 8 May 2023)

Spink, K (1997) *Mother Teresa* Harper One, San Francisco, US

Startrek.com (2023) *Star Trek* Available at www.startrek.com (Accessed 5 May 2023)

Starwars.com (2023) *Star Wars* Available at www.starwars.com (Accessed 5 May 2023)

Suzuki, D T (1957) *Mysticism – Christian and Buddhist* Harper and Brothers, New York, US

Syed, M (2022) *A million children abused by Italian priests, and it barely makes the news*

Available at www.the times.co.uk (Accessed 8 May 2023)

Vermes, G (2011) *The Complete Dead Sea Scrolls in English* Penguin Classics, London, UK

Vogel, G (2021) *Unethical? Unnecessary? The Covid-19 vaccine booster debate intensifies* Available at www.science.org (Accessed 8 May 2023)

Warnerbros.co.uk (2023) *The Wizard of Oz* Available at www.Warnerbros.co.uk (Accessedon 8 May 2023)

Weiss, B (1988) *Many Lives, Many Masters* Simon and Schuster, New York, US.

Weiss, S (2021)What do Jews believe about the afterlife? Jerusalem Post, Available at https://m.jpost.com (Accessed 5 May 2023)

Williamson, H R (2006) *The Challenge of Bernadette* Gracewing Publishing, Leominster, England.

Wolpert, S (2002) *Gandhi's Passion: The life and legacy of Mahatma Gandhi* Oxford University Press, Oxford, UK.

www.ingramcontent.com/pod-product-compliance
Lightning Source LLC
Chambersburg PA
CBHW052137070526
44585CB00017B/1867